STUDY GUIDE

MODERN MANAGEMENT

STUDY GUIDE

MODERN MANAGEMENT
Ninth Edition

SAMUEL C. CERTO

Andrew P. Yap
Florida International University

Upper Saddle River, New Jersey 07458

Acquisitions editor: David Shafer
Assistant editor: Melanie Olsen
Production editor: Carol Zaino
Manufacturer: Courier, Bookmart Press

Copyright ©2003 by Prentice-Hall, Inc., Upper Saddle River, New Jersey, 07458. All rights reserved. Printed in the United States of America. This publication is protected by copyright, and permission should be obtained from the publisher prior to any prohibited reproduction, storage in a retrieval system, or transmission in any form or by any means, electronic, mechanical, photocopying, recording, or likewise. For information regarding permission(s), write to: Rights and Permissions Department.

ISBN 0-13-009660-1

10 9 8 7 6 5

Table of Contents

Chapter 1 - Modern Management: A Digital Focus 1

Chapter 2 – Managing: History and Current Thinking 10

Chapter 3 – Corporate Social Responsibility and Business Ethics 19

Chapter 4 – Management and Diversity 29

Chapter 5 – Managing in the Global Arena 39

Chapter 6 – Principles of Planning 49

Chapter 7 – Making Decisions 60

Chapter 8 – Strategic Planning 69

Chapter 9 – Plans and Planning Tools 79

Chapter 10 – Fundamentals of Organizing 88

Chapter 11 – Responsibility, Authority, and Delegation 96

Chapter 12 – Managing Human Resources 106

Chapter 13 – Organizational Change and Stress 115

Chapter 14 – Fundamentals of Influencing and Communication 124

Chapter 15 – Leadership 132

Chapter 16 – Motivation 141

Chapter 17 – Groups, Teams, and Corporate Culture 150

Chapter 18 – Understanding People: Attitudes, Perception, and Learning 159

Chapter 19 – Principles of Controlling 168

Chapter 20 – Production Management and Control 176

Chapter 21 – Information Technology and the Internet 188

Chapter 22 – Competitiveness: Quality and Innovation 198

Chapter 23 – Management's Digital Dimension 208

STUDENT STUDY GUIDE

Modern Management
Samuel C. Certo
Ninth Edition

INTRODUCTION

The purpose of this study guide is to assist you in more effectively learning the material in *Modern Management* by Samuel C. Certo.

The study guide is designed and written to reinforce your learning from the textbook, class lectures, and class discussions. The objectives of this study guide are:

1. to provide you with the materials that will be useful in learning the business vocabulary and business concepts presented in your text.

2. to provide you with an opportunity to test your understanding of what you have read, studied, and learned.

3. to help you prepare for quizzes and examinations by testing yourself with sample exam-type questions.

4. to encourage you to apply your understanding of the business concepts presented in the text to interesting, real-world business problems and opportunities.

I hope that this study guide will help with your exam preparation, case analyses, and overall learning of the concepts of management. Good luck and enjoy the course!

Andrew P. Yap
Florida International University
Miami, Florida

Modern Management (9th ed.)
Part 1 – Introduction to Management
Chapter One - Modern Management: A Digital Focus

Overview

The first chapter provides an overview of the importance of management, and an introduction to the roles of management, including: several ways to define management, a presentation of its basic functions, working definitions of managerial effectiveness and efficiency, an exploration of management skills and its universality, and an explanation of career management.

Chapter Outline

Introductory Case: Lands' End Management - Learning How to Use the Web

I. THE IMPORTANCE OF MANAGEMENT

    A. Managers influence all phases of modern organizations.

II. THE MANAGEMENT TASK

    A. The Role of Management

    The role of managers is to guide organizations toward goal accomplishment.

    B. Defining Management

    Management is the process of reaching organizational goals by working with and through people and other organizational resources.

    C. The Management Process: Management Functions

    Management functions are activities that make up the management process.

    The four basic management functions:
    1. Planning
       Planning activity focuses on attaining goals.
    2. Organizing
       Organizing assigns planning's tasks and then creates a mechanism to put plans into action.
    3. Influencing
       Influencing can be defined as guiding the activities of organization members in appropriate directions. It is also commonly referred to as *motivating, leading, directing,* or *actuating*.
    4. Controlling
       Controlling is where managers:
       a) Gather information that measures recent performance
       b) Compare present to preestablished performance
       c) Determine if the organization should be modified to meet preestablished standards

    D. Management Process and Goal Attainment
       1. To be effective, a manager must understand how the four management functions are practiced, not simply how they are defined and related.

E. Management and Organizational Resources

Organizational Resources are all assets available for activation during normal operations, and they include:
1. human resources - the people who work for an organization
2. monetary resources - amounts of money that managers use to purchase goods and services for the organization
3. raw materials resources - ingredients used directly in the manufacturing of products
4. capital resources - machines used during the manufacturing process

F. Managerial effectiveness

Managerial effectiveness refers to management's use of organizational resources in meeting organizational goals.

1. Managerial efficiency
Managerial efficiency is the degree to which organizational resources contribute to productivity. It is measured by the proportion of total organizational resources used during the production process.

2. Management Skills
   a) **Technical skills** are skills involving the ability to apply specialized knowledge and expertise to work-related techniques and procedures.
   b) **Human skills** are skills involving the ability to build cooperation within the team being led.
   c) **Conceptual skills** are skills involving the ability to see the organization as a whole.

III. THE UNIVERSALITY OF MANAGEMENT

Management principles are universal. **Universality of management** means that the principles of management are applicable to all types of organizations and organizational levels.

A. The Theory of Characteristics

All managers should possess certain characteristics, such as positive physical and mental qualities and special knowledge related to the specific operation.

IV. MANAGEMENT CAREERS

A. A Definition of Career

A **career** is a sequence of work-related positions occupied by a person over the course of a lifetime.

B. Career Stages, Life Stages, and Performance
1. Exploration Stage
The **exploration stage** is the first stage in career evolution; it occurs at the beginning of a career, when the individual is typically 15 to 25 years of age, and it is characterized by self-analysis and the exploration of different types of available jobs.

2. Establishment Stage
   The **establishment stage** is the second stage in career evolution; individuals of about 25 to 45 years of age typically start to become more productive, or higher performers.
3. Maintenance Stage
   The **maintenance stage** is the third stage in career evolution; individuals of about 45 to 65 years of age either become more productive, stabilize, or become less productive.
   Career plateauing is a period of little or no apparent progress in the growth of a career.
4. Decline Stage
   The **decline stage** is the fourth and last stage in career evolution; it occurs near retirement age, when individuals of about 65 years of age show declining productivity.

C. Promoting Your Own Career

The careful formulation and implementation of appropriate tactics can enhance the success of a management career.

D. Special Career Issues

   1. Women Managers
   2. Dual-Career Couples
      a) How Dual-Career Couples Cope
   3. Modern Management's Digital Focus
      a) Defining Digital Dimension
         Digital pertains to components related to the Internet and Internet-supporting technologies like voice recognition or wireless technologies.
         A **digital dimension** is that segment of management that focuses on meeting management challenges through the application of the Internet and Internet-supportive technologies.
         Digital dimensioning is the process of determining and using a unique combination of Internet and Internet-supportive tools that best help management meet organizational challenges and thereby enhance organizational goal attainment.
      b) Digital Dimensioning and Traditional Management Functions

V. SPECIAL FEATURES FOR REMAINING CHAPTERS

The **law of the situation** indicates that managers must continually analyze the unique circumstances within their organizations and apply management concepts to fit those circumstances.

A. Spotlights

   1. Global Spotlight
   2. Ethics Spotlight
   3. Diversity Spotlight
   4. Quality Spotlight
   5. People Spotlight

B. Across Industries

C. Digital Focus

Chapter One - Modern Management: A Digital Focus

Test Your Knowledge

Essay

1. Discuss the importance of management to society and to individuals. (p. 4)

2. Describe the role of management in an organization. (p. 6)

3. Discuss managerial effectiveness and managerial efficiency. (p. 9)

4. Discuss the universality of management. (p. 11)

5. What is meant by modern management's digital dimension? (p. 15)

True-False

T F 1. Our society could neither exist as we know it today nor improve without a steady stream of managers to guide its organizations. (p. 4)

T F 2. Management has no meaning apart from its goals. (p. 6)

T F 3. One of the four basic types of organizational resources is raw materials. (p. 8)

T F 4. If an organization is using its resources to attain its goals, the organization's managers are efficient. (p. 9)

T F 5. Managerial effectiveness is the degree to which organizational resources contribute to productivity. (p. 9)

T F 6. Technical skills are skills involving the ability to see the organization as a whole. (p. 11)

T F 7. The statement that management principles are universal means that they apply to all types of organizations and organizational levels. (p. 11)

T F 8. The universality of management means that the principles of management are applicable to all types of organizations and organizational levels. (p. 11)

T F 9. Women are well-represented in management today. (p. 14)

T F 10. Women are more likely to be sexually harassed in the workplace than men. (p. 15)

Multiple Choice

1. Managers influence _____ phases of modern organizations. (p. 4)
   a. all
   b. some
   c. a few
   d. no

Chapter One - Modern Management: A Digital Focus

2. Prospective managers need to _____. (p. 4)
   a. understand the significance of managerial work to themselves and society
   b. understand its related benefits
   c. know what the management task entails
   d. all of the above

3. Government statistics show that management positions have increased from _____ percent to _____ percent of all jobs since 1950. (p. 4)
   a. 5, 10
   b. 10, 18
   c. 18, 24
   d. none of the above

4. In the long term, managerial positions can yield _____. (p. 5)
   a. high salaries and status
   b. interesting work and personal growth
   c. intense feelings of accomplishment
   d. all of the above

5. The role of managers is to guide organizations toward _____. (p. 6)
   a. human resources
   b. planning
   c. goal accomplishment
   d. none of the above

6. Management can refer to _____. (p. 6)
   a. the process that managers follow in order to accomplish organizational goals
   b. a body of knowledge; in this context, management is a cumulative body of information that furnishes insights on how to manage
   c. the individuals who guide and direct organizations or to a career devoted to the task of guiding and directing organizations
   d. all of the above

7. Which of the following is not a function of management? (p. 7)
   a. Directing
   b. Influencing
   c. Organizing
   d. Planning

8. Planning involves _____. (p. 7)
   a. choosing tasks that must be performed to attain organizational goals
   b. outlining how the tasks must be performed
   c. indicating when they should be performed
   d. all of the above

9. Organizing _____. (p. 7)
   a. assigns planning's tasks to various individuals or groups within the organization
   b. creates a mechanism to put plans into action
   c. a and b
   d. none of the above

Chapter One - Modern Management: A Digital Focus

10. Influencing, one of the four management functions, is commonly referred to as _____. (p. 7)
    a. motivating
    b. leading
    c. directing
    d. all of the above

11. Controlling is an _____ process. (p. 8)
    a. ongoing
    b. seasonal
    c. year-end
    d. quarterly

12. Which of the following are organizational resources? (p. 8)
    a. Human
    b. Monetary
    c. Capital
    d. All of the above

13. Management's use of organizational resources in meeting organizational goals is _____. (p. 9)
    a. efficiency
    b. productivity
    c. effectiveness
    d. none are correct

14. Managerial effectiveness exists on a continuum ranging from _____ to _____. (p. 9)
    a. ineffective, effective
    b. effective, ineffective
    c. inefficient, efficient
    d. efficient, inefficient

15. _____ means that a very small proportion of total resources contributes to productivity during the manufacturing process. (p. 9)
    a. Ineffective
    b. Inefficient
    c. Effective
    d. Efficient

16. Skills that are important for successful management performance are _____. (p. 10)
    a. Technical
    b. Human
    c. Conceptual
    d. All of the above

17. Skills that involve the ability to apply specialized knowledge and expertise are called what? (p. 10)
    a. Human
    b. Technical
    c. Conceptual
    d. Kinetic

18. What is the first stage of a career? (p. 12)
    a. Exploration
    b. Decline
    c. Stable state
    d. None is correct

19. In the maintenance stage, individuals show _____. (p. 13)
    a. career growth
    b. career maintenance
    c. career stagnation
    d. all of the above

20. In the establishment stage, individuals are _____ years of age. (p. 13)
    a. 15 to 25
    b. 25 to 45
    c. 45 to 65
    d. none of the above

21. Tom Peters predicts that _____. (p. 15)
    a. networks of relationships will replace rigid organizational structures
    b. star workers will be replaced by teams of workers empowered to make decisions
    c. detailed rules and procedures will be replaced by a flexible system that calls for judgments based on key values and a constant search for new ways to get the job done
    d. all of the above

22. The strengths of _____ (that are often attributed to women) will be the dominant virtues in the corporation of the future. (p. 15)
    a. emphasizing interrelationships
    b. listening
    c. motivating others
    d. all of the above

23. Digital dimensioning can impact _____. (p. 16)
    a. planning and organizing
    b. influencing and controlling
    c. a and b
    d. none of the above

24. The law of the _____ indicates that managers must continually analyze the unique circumstances within their organizations and apply management concepts to fit those circumstances. (p. 17)
    a. occasion
    b. situation
    c. organization
    d. none of the above

25. _____ is defined as differences in people such as age, gender, ethnicity, nationality, and ability. (p. 17)
    a. Multiethnic
    b. Politically correct language
    c. Diversity
    d. None of the above

Chapter One - Modern Management: A Digital Focus

Fill-In

1. _____ is important to society. (p. 4)

2. Management is the process of reaching organizational _____ by working with and through people and other organizational resources. (p. 7)

3. _____ activity focuses on attaining goals. (p. 7)

4. Managerial _____ is the proportion of total organizational resources that contribute to productivity during the manufacturing process. (p. 9)

5. As one moves from lower-level management to upper-level management, _____ skills become more important and _____ skills less important. However, _____ skills remain extremely important. (p. 11)

6. A _____ is a sequence of work-related positions. (p. 12)

7. Individuals tend to show the first significant increase in performance during the _____ career stage. (p. 13)

8. Career _____ is a period of little or no apparent progress in the growth of a career. (p. 13)

9. Savings institutions and financial firms tend to have the _____ percentage of women officers. (p. 14)

10. The trucking, semiconductor, and waste management industries have the _____ percentage of women officers. (p. 14)

Chapter One - Modern Management: A Digital Focus

Answers

Essay

1. Managers influence all phases of modern organizations. Plant mangers run manufacturing operations, sales managers maintain a sales force that markets goods, and personnel managers provide organizations with a competent and productive workforce.

2. Essentially, the role of managers is to guide organizations toward goal accomplishment. All organizations exist for certain purposes or goals, and managers are responsible for combining and using organizational resources to ensure that their organizations achieve their purposes. Management moves an organization toward its purposes or goals by assigning activities that organization members perform.

3. As managers use their resources, they must strive to be both effective and efficient. **Managerial effectiveness** refers to management's use of organizational resources in meeting organizational goals. **Managerial efficiency** is the proportion of total organizational resources that contribute to productivity during the manufacturing process. The higher this proportion, the more inefficient the manager.

4. **Universality of management** means that the principles of management are applicable to all types of organizations and organizational levels. Management principles are universal and managers' jobs vary somewhat from one type of organization to anther because each organizational type requires the use of specialized knowledge, exists in a unique working and political environment, and uses different technology.

5. **Digital dimensioning** is the process of determining and using a unique combination of Internet and Internet-supportive tools that best help management meet organizational challenges and thereby enhance organizational goal attainment. Fundamentally, the focus of management's digital dimension is on employing the Internet and related technologies to maximize organizational goal attainment.

True-False

1. T	3. T	5. F	7. T	9. F
2. T	4. F	6. F	8. T	10. T

Multiple Choice

1. a	6. d	11. a	16. d	21. d
2. d	7. a	12. d	17. b	22. d
3. b	8. d	13. c	18. a	23. c
4. d	9. c	14. a	19. d	24. b
5. c	10. d	15. b	20. b	25. c

Fill-In

1. Management
2. goals
3. Planning
4. efficiency
5. conceptual, technical, human
6. career
7. establishment
8. plateauing
9. highest
10. lowest

Modern Management (9th ed.)
Part 1 – Introduction to Management
Chapter Two – Managing: History and Current Thinking

Overview

This chapter explores and explains the history of management as well as new approaches. It provides an appreciation for traditional classical management and its founders. The behavioral approach, the human relations movement, management science, and the new triangular and contingency approaches to management will also be introduced.

Chapter Outline

Introductory Case: A Problem at McDonald's

I. THE CLASSICAL APPROACH

   The **classical approach** is the management approach that emphasizes organizational efficiency to increase organizational success.

   A. Lower-Level Management Analysis

      1. Lower-level management analysis concentrates on the "one best way" approach to perform a task.
      2. This "one best way" approach became known as scientific management.
      3. Proponents of scientific management are Taylor, the Gilbreths, and Gantt.

   B. Comprehensive Management Analysis

      1. This approach involves studying the management function as a whole.
      2. Proponents of this approach are Fayol and his fourteen principles, Chester Barnard, and others who greatly influenced early management approaches.

   C. Limits to the Classical Approach

      1. The Classical Approach did not adequately emphasize the human variables in the organization.
      2. Critical interpersonal areas were shortchanged in the classical approach.

II. THE BEHAVIORAL APPROACH

   The **behavioral approach** is a management approach that emphasizes increasing organizational success by focusing on human variables within the organization. The Hawthorne Studies are keys to this approach.

   A. The behavioral approach is usually described as beginning with a series of studies conducted between 1924 and 1932, which investigated the behavior and attitudes of workers at the Hawthorne (Chicago) Works of the Western Electric Company.

   B. The **human relations movement** is a people-oriented approach to management in which the interaction of people in organizations is studied to judge its impact on organizational success.

Chapter Two – Managing: History and Current Thinking

III. THE MANAGEMENT SCIENCE APPROACH

The **management science approach** is a management approach that emphasizes the use of the scientific method and quantitative techniques to increase organizational success.

A. The beginning of the management science approach, or operations research, came from the World War II period where leading scientists were asked to help solve complex problems in the military.

B. The Characteristics of the Management Science Applications

   1. There are four (4) primary characteristics: analysis of a large number of variables; use of economic implications as guidelines; the use of mathematical models; and the use of computers.

IV. THE CONTINGENCY APPROACH

The **contingency approach** to management is a management approach that emphasizes that what managers do in practice depends on a given set of circumstances—a situation.

A. Main challenges of using the contingency approach

   1. Perceiving organizational situations as they actually exist
   2. Choosing the management tactics best suited to those situations
   3. Competently implementing those tactics

V. THE SYSTEMS APPROACH

The **systems approach** is a management approach based on general system theory—the theory that to understand fully the operation of an entity, the entity must be viewed as a system. This requires understanding the interdependence of its parts.

A. The types of systems within systems analysis are open and closed. The open system is one that is influenced by and constantly interacts with its environment while a closed system does not.

B. Systems and Wholeness

   1. The concept of wholeness is important because the system is viewed as a whole and modified only through changes to its parts.

C. The Management System

   1. The management system is an open system whose major parts are organizational input, organizational process, and organizational output.

D. Information for Management Systems Analysis

   1. **Triangular management** is a management approach that emphasizes using information from the classical, behavioral and management science schools of thought to manage the open management system.

F. Learning Organization: A New Approach?

The Learning Organization is an organization that does well in creating, acquiring, and transferring knowledge, and in modifying behavior to reflect new knowledge.

1. According to Peter Senge, building a learning organization entails building five features within an organization: (1) system thinking, (2) shared vision, (3) challenging of mental models, (4) team learning, (5) personal mastery.

Test Your Knowledge

Essay

1. Discuss the behavioral approach to management. What two studies were important to the development of the behavioral approach to management? (p. 31)

2. Discuss the four primary characteristics that are usually present in situations in which management science techniques are applied. (p. 35)

3. Compare the differences between a closed system and an open system. Give a specific example of each to support your answer. (p. 36)

4. List the six guidelines, according to L. Thomas Hopkins, that should be followed by anyone doing systems analysis. (p. 37)

5. Define the concept of a learning organization and list the five features needed to build a learning organization within an organization. (p. 39)

True-False

T F   1. The classical approach to management emphasizes efficiency to increase organizational success. (p. 26)

T F   2. Scientific management focuses on myriad ways to perform a task. (p. 27)

T F   3. Frederick Taylor is often called the father of scientific management. (p. 28)

T F   4. The Gilbreths used motion studies in their research. (p. 28)

T F   5. Scheduling is key to Gantt's approach to management. (p. 29)

T F   6. The Hawthorne Studies are key to understanding scientific management. (p. 31)

T F   7. Quantitative techniques are important to the management science approach. (p. 34)

T F   8. The contingency approach is based on the situation in which a manager finds her or himself. (p. 35)

T F   9. An open system is constantly interacting with its environment. (p. 36)

T F   10. Triangular management uses sophisticated math formulas to assess management approaches. (p. 38)

Chapter Two – Managing: History and Current Thinking

Multiple Choice

1. Which of following is *not* one of the three basic approaches to management? (p. 26)
   a. Classical
   b. Qualitative
   c. Behavioral
   d. Management science

2. The _____ to management is a management approach that emphasizes organizational efficiency to increase organizational success. (p. 26)
   a. classical approach
   b. qualitative approach
   c. behavioral approach
   d. management science approach

3. Which of the following approaches to management was the product of the first concentrated effort to develop a body of management thought? (p. 26)
   a. qualitative approach
   b. behavioral approach
   c. classical approach
   d. management science approach

4. _____ emphasizes the "one best way" to perform a task. (p. 27)
   a. Behavioral management
   b. Scientific management
   c. Classical management
   d. Cultural management

5. All of the following were major contributors to the scientific methods of management EXCEPT: (p. 27)
   a. Taylor
   b. Gilbreths
   c. Gantt
   d. Fayol

6. Which of the following general principles of management, suggested by Fayol, emphasizes that work would be divided among individuals and groups to ensure that effort and attention are focused on special portions of the task? (p. 30)
   a. division of work
   b. authority
   c. discipline
   d. unity of command

7. Who of the following was the major contributor to the comprehensive analysis of management? (p. 30)
   a. Taylor
   b. Gilbreths
   c. Gantt
   d. Fayol

8. Which of the following is seen as a limitation to classical management? (p. 31)
   a. It is too oriented toward behavior.
   b. It does not adequately emphasize human variation.
   c. It is not efficiency-oriented enough.
   d. None is correct

9. The _____ to management emphasizes increasing production through an understanding of people. (p. 31)
   a. quantitative approach
   b. behavioral approach
   c. classical approach
   d. management science approach

10. The Hawthorne Studies begin our knowledge of what is termed _____. (p. 31)
    a. the qualitative approach
    b. the learning approach
    c. the quantitative approach
    d. the behavioral approach

11. The human relations movement is a _____-oriented approach. (p. 33)
    a. public
    b. public relations
    c. people
    d. task

12. _____ is the ability to work with people in a way that enhances organizational success. (p. 33)
    a. Scientific management
    b. Human relations skill
    c. Operations management
    d. Technological skill

13. The _____ is a management approach that emphasizes the use of the scientific method and quantitative techniques to increase organizational success. (p. 34)
    a. human relations approach
    b. management science approach
    c. behavioral management approach
    d. contingency approach to management

14. Another term for management science is what? (p. 34)
    a. Operations research
    b. Management search
    c. Behavior quantified
    d. None are correct

15. Which of the following is a management approach emphasizing that what managers do in practice depends on a given set of circumstances? (p. 35)
    a. human relations approach
    b. management science approach
    c. behavioral management approach
    d. contingency approach to management

Chapter Two – Managing: History and Current Thinking

16. Which of the following awards is linked with quality standards? (p. 35)
    a. Emelie
    b. Baldrige
    c. Markey
    d. None are correct

17. You are managing a new organization and you observe certain types of interaction among the employees and decide how to approach the situation. What type of management approach are you employing? (p. 35)
    a. Contingency
    b. Behavioral
    c. Fayolian
    d. Scientific

18. A _____ is a number of interdependent parts functioning as a whole for some purpose. (p. 36)
    a. system
    b. procedure
    c. policy
    d. plan

19. Which of the following types of stems is one that is not influenced by, and does not interact with, its environment? (p. 36)
    a. open system
    b. closed system
    c. organic system
    d. turbulent system

20. A(n) _____ is one that is influenced by, and is continually interacting with, its environment. (p. 36)
    a. open system
    b. closed system
    c. mechanistic system
    d. fixed system

21. What is the systems approach based on? (p. 36)
    a. General systems theory
    b. Copernican theory
    c. Mathematical qualitative systems
    d. None are correct

22. A management _____ is composed of a number of parts that function interdependently to achieve a purpose. (p. 37)
    a. system
    b. function
    c. theory
    d. None are correct

23. All of the following are major parts of the management system EXCEPT: (p. 37)
    a. organizational input.
    b. organizational process.
    c. organizational output.
    d. all of the selections are major parts of the management system.

24. _____ is a management approach that emphasizes using information from the classical, behavioral, and management science schools of thought to manage the open management system. (p. 38)
    a. Secular management
    b. Triangular management
    c. Circular management
    d. Standardized management

25. An organization that does well in creating, acquiring, and transferring knowledge, and in modifying behavior to reflect new knowledge is called a(n) _____. (p. 39)
    a. learning organization.
    b. triangular organization.
    c. bureaucratic organization.
    d. virtual organization.

Fill-In

1. Lower-level management analysis concentrates on the _____ to perform a task; that is, it investigates how a task situation can be structured to get the highest production from workers. (p. 27)

2. The primary investigative tool in the Gilbreths' research _____, which consists of reducing each job to the most basic movement possible. (p. 28)

3. Because of his writings on the elements and general principles of management, _____ is usually regarded as the pioneer of administrative theory. (p. 30)

4. The _____ has made some important contributions to the study and practice of management. Advocates of this approach to management have continually stressed the need to use humane methods in managing people. (p. 33)

5. The _____ approach suggests that managers can best improve their organizations by using the scientific method and mathematical techniques to solve operational problems. (p. 34)

6. In general, the _____ attempts to outline the conditions or situations in which various management methods have the best chance of success. (p. 36)

7. _____ integrates the knowledge of various specialized fields so that the system as a whole can be better understood. (p. 36)

8. The management system is a(n) _____ -- that is, one that interacts with its environment. (p. 37)

9. The use of the classical approach, behavioral approach, and management science (p. 38)
   approach to management to analyze the management system is referred to as _____.

10. A new approach to management that is evolving to handle the new range of issues facing (p. 39)
    today's managers is called the _____.

Answers

Essay

1. The behavioral approach to management emphasizes increasing production through an understanding of people. According to proponents of this approach, if managers understand their people and adapt their organizations to them, organizational success will usually follow. The Hawthorne Studies and the Human Relations Movement were important to the development of the behavioral approach to management.

2. First, the management problems studied are so complicated that managers need help in analyzing a large number of variables. Second, a management science application generally uses economic implications as guidelines for making a particular decision. Third, the use of mathematical models to investigate the decision situation is typical in management science applications. The fourth characteristic of a management science application is the use of computers. The great complexity of managerial problems and the sophisticated mathematical analysis of problem-related information required are two factors that make computers very valuable to the management science analyst.

3. Closed systems are not influenced by, and do not interact with, their environments. They are mostly mechanical and have predetermined motions or activities that must be performed regardless of the environment. A clock is an example of a closed system. Regardless of its environment, a clock's wheels and gears must function in a predetermined way if the clock as a whole is to exist and serve its purpose. The second type of system, the open system, is continually interacting with its environment. A plant is an example of an open system. Constant interaction with the environment influences the plant's state of existence and its future.

4. The six guidelines that should be followed include:
   a. The whole should be the main focus of analysis, with the parts receiving secondary attention
   b. Integration is the key variable in wholeness analysis. It is defined as the interrelatedness of the many parts within the whole.
   c. Possible modifications in each part should be weighed in relation to possible effects on every other part.
   d. Each part has some role to perform so that the whole can accomplish its purpose.
   e. The nature of the part and its function is determined by its position in the whole.
   f. All analysis starts with the existence of the whole. The parts and their interrelationships should then evolve to best suite the purpose of the whole.

5. A learning organization is an organization that does well in creating, acquiring, and transferring knowledge, and in modifying behavior to reflect new knowledge. The five features needed to build a learning organization within an organization are: (1) systems thinking, (2) shared vision, (3) challenging of metal models, (4) team learning, and (5) personal mastery.

True-False

1. T
2. F
3. T
4. T
5. T
6. F
7. T
8. T
9. T
10. F

Multiple Choice

1. b
2. a
3. c
4. b
5. c
6. a
7. d
8. b
9. b
10. d
11. c
12. b
13. b
14. a
15. d
16. b
17. a
18. a
19. b
20. a
21. a
22. a
23. d
24. b
25. a

Fill-In

1. "one best way"
2. motion study
3. Henri Fayol
4. human relations movement
5. management science
6. contingency approach
7. General system theory
8. open system
9. triangular management
10. learning organization approach

Modern Management (9th ed.)
Part 2 – Modern Management Challenges
Chapter Three – Corporate Social Responsibility and Business Ethics

Overview

The chapter provides you with an overview of corporate social responsibility and business ethics from a conceptual as well as justification standpoint. Strategies are presented and discussed as well as how the concept impacts the basic functions of management. A discussion of the relationship between ethics and management as well as how to incorporate ethics into the practice of management is also included.

Chapter Outline

Introductory Case: IBM Uses Web Site to Promote Social Responsibility Goals

I. FUNDAMENTALS OF SOCIAL RESPONSIBILITY

Corporate Social Responsibility (CSR) is the managerial obligation to take action that protects and improves both the welfare of society as a whole and the interests of the organization. There are many models of CSR.

A. The *Davis* Model of CSR—The model presents five propositions that describe why and how businesses should adhere to the obligation to take action that protects and improves the welfare of society as well as the organization.

1. Proposition 1: Social responsibility arises from social power;
2. Proposition 2: Businesses shall operate as a two-way open system, with open receipt of inputs from society and open disclosure to it operations to the public;
3. Proposition 3: The social costs and benefits of an activity, product, or service shall be thoroughly calculated and considered whether to proceed with it;
4. Proposition 4: The social costs related to each activity, product, or service shall be passed on to the consumer;
5. Proposition 5: Business institutions, as citizens, have the responsibility to become involved in certain social problems that are outside their normal areas of operation.

B. Areas of Corporate Social Responsibility

1. There are many areas where CSR may be able to act to protect and improve the welfare of society, including environmental affairs, urban affairs, consumer affairs, and employment practices.

C. Varying Options for Social Responsibility

1. Arguments *for* Business Performing SR Activities begin with the premise that business as a whole is a subset of society, one that exerts a significant impact on the way society exists.

2. Arguments *against* Business Performing SR Activities include Milton Friedman's theory that the business of business is business so business must stay within the law, but need not go beyond this to be socially responsible. Freedman argues that if business is socially responsible, this could lead to its demise.

D. Conclusions about the Performance of Social Responsibility Activities by Business

    1. Three basic guidelines that are generally used to determine social responsibility include: (1) perform all legally required socially responsible activities; (2) consider voluntarily performing social responsibility activities beyond those legally required; and (3) inform all relevant individuals of the extent to which their organization will become involved in performing social responsibility activities.

II. SOCIAL RESPONSIVENESS (SR)

Social responsiveness is the degree of effectiveness and efficiency an organization displays in pursuing its social responsibility.

A. There are three areas of concern: (1) determining if a social responsibility exists; (2) social responsiveness and decision-making; and (3) approaches to meeting social responsibilities.

    1. Determining if a social responsibility exists: managers assess business and also keep the stakeholders in mind. **Stakeholders** are all individuals and groups that are directly or indirectly affected by an organization's decision.

    2. Social responsiveness and decision-making as it impacts the effective and efficient use of an organization's resources.

    3. Approaches to meeting social responsibilities does the following to meet social obligations: (1) incorporates social goals into the annual planning process; (2) seeks comparative industry norms for social programs; and (3) presents reports to organization members, the board of directors, and stockholders on social responsibility progress.

    4. Sethi presents three approaches to meeting social obligations: (1) social obligation approach; (2) social responsibility approach; and (3) social responsiveness approach.

III. SOCIAL RESPONSIBILITY ACTIVITIES AND MANAGEMENT FUNCTIONS

A. Planning SR Activities includes the overall planning process, such as scanning the environment for information.

B. Organizing Social Responsibility Activities

C. Influencing Individuals Performing Social Responsibility Activities

D. Controlling Social Responsibility Activities including areas of measurement and social audits.

    1. All companies should take social responsibility measurements in at least the following four major areas: (1) the economic function area, (2) the quality-of-life area, (3) the social investment area, and (4) the problem-solving area.

Chapter Three – Corporate Social Responsibility and Business Ethics

IV. HOW SOCIETY CAN HELP BUSINESS MEET SOCIAL OBLIGATIONS

   A. There are a number of ways that business can meet social obligations. Among them are:

      1. Set rules that are clear and consistent
      2. Keep the rules technically feasible
      3. Make sure the rules are economically feasible
      4. Make the rules prospective, not retroactive
      5. Make the rules goal-setting, not procedure-prescribing

V. BUSINESS ETHICS

   A. Definition of Ethics: our concern for good behavior; our obligation to consider not only our own personal well-being but also that of other human beings.

      1. Business ethics involves the capacity to reflect on values in the corporate decision-making process, to determine how these values and decisions affect various stakeholder groups, and to establish how managers can use these observations in day-to-day company management.

   B. WHY ETHICS IS A VITAL PART OF MANAGEMENT PRACTICES

      1. Productivity—what is the relationship of ethics and productivity?
      2. Stakeholder Relations—who are the shareholders? How does management coordinate all the different shareholder demands?
      3. Government Regulations—what is the impact of government relations on ethics?

   C. A CODE OF ETHICS

   Definition of a code of ethics: a formal statement that acts as a guide for making decisions and acting within the organization.

   D. CREATING AN ETHICAL WORKPLACE

      1. Relevant ethical standards include all of the following: (1) the golden rule; (2) the utilitarian principle; (3) Kant's categorical imperative; (4) the professional ethic; (5) the TV test; (6) the legal test; and (7) the four-way test.

Test Your Knowledge

Essay

1. List and discuss the five propositions, according to Keith Davis, that describe why and how business should adhere to the obligation to take action that protects and improves the welfare of society as well as of the organization. (p. 49)

2. Discuss the three sequential phases involved in converting social responsibility policies into appropriate action. (p. 58)

3. List and discuss the four major areas in which all companies should take social responsibility measurements. (p. 61)

Chapter Three – Corporate Social Responsibility and Business Ethics

4. Identify the five responsibilities that society has to business according to Jerry McAfee, chairman of the board and CEO of Gulf Oil corporation. (p. 62)

5. A potential action would be considered ethical by the general public if it is consistent with one or more standards. List and discuss five of these standards. (p. 66)

True-False

T F 1. There really is no such thing as corporate social responsibility according to some thinkers. (p. 50)

T F 2. Davis argues that social responsibility arises from social power. (p. 49)

T F 3. Milton Friedman believes that the tenets of social responsibility set up a conflict of interest for business. (p. 51)

T F 4. Federal legislation requires that businesses perform certain social responsibility activities. (p. 52)

T F 5. Companies sometimes voluntarily perform social responsibility acts. (p. 52)

T F 6. One negative outcome of social responsibility can be increased short-term as well as decreased short-term profitability. (p. 52)

T F 7. Stakeholder is really just another name for stockholder. (p. 55)

T F 8. In a social obligation approach the company considers business to have societal and economic goals as well as obligations to anticipate potential social problems. (p. 57)

T F 9. A policy provides guidelines. (p. 58)

T F 10. Unfortunately, social responsibility cannot be measured in an audit like money can. (p. 60)

Multiple Choice

1. What is defined in the following: a managerial obligation to take action that protects and improves both the welfare of society as a whole and the interests of the organization. (p. 48)
   a. Ethics
   b. Social ethics
   c. Corporate social ethics
   d. Corporate social responsibility

2. Davis provides which of the following as a guides to social responsibility? (p. 49)
   a. Social responsibility arises from social power
   b. Business shall operate a two-way open system
   c. Business institutions have the responsibility to become involved in certain social problems
   d. All are correct

Chapter Three – Corporate Social Responsibility and Business Ethics

3. Who of the following opposes social responsibility if it goes beyond the legal demands on the company? (p. 51)
   a. Lipton
   b. Davis
   c. Friedman
   d. None of the above

4. _____ are all individuals and groups that are directly or indirectly affected by an organizations decisions. (p. 55)
   a. Stakeholders
   b. Suppliers
   c. Stockholders
   d. Competitors

5. Which of the following defines social responsiveness? (p. 55)
   a. Degree of effectiveness and efficiency an organization displays in pursuing its social responsibility
   b. All individuals and groups who practice social responsibility
   c. Meeting social and economic goals equally
   d. None of the above

6. The _____ approach is an approach to meeting social obligation that considers business to have primarily economic purposes and confines social responsibility activity largely to conformance to existing legislation. (p. 57)
   a. social responsibility
   b. social obligation
   c. social responsiveness
   d. social capitalism

7. Which of the following is an approach to meeting social obligations that considers business as having both societal and economic goals? (p. 57)
   a. the social responsibility approach
   b. the social obligation approach
   c. the social responsiveness approach
   d. the social capitalism approach

8. The _____ approach is an approach to meeting social obligations that considers business to have societal and economic goals as well as the obligation to anticipate potential social problems and to work actively toward preventing them from occurring. (p. 57)
   a. social responsibility
   b. social obligation
   c. social responsiveness
   d. social capitalism

9. Which of the following are aspects of environmental forecasts? (p. 58)
   a. Social issues
   b. Economic issues
   c. Political issues
   d. All the above

10. A _____ is a management tool that furnishes broad guidelines from channeling management thinking in specific directions. (p. 58)
    a. procedure
    b. policy
    c. ethics
    d. budget

11. All companies should take social responsibility measurements, at a minimum, in all of the following areas EXCEPT: (p. 61)
    a. the technological area
    b. the economic function area
    c. the quality-of-life area
    d. the social investment area

12. A(n) _____ is the process of measuring the present social responsibility activities of an organization. (p. 61)
    a. social audit
    b. social procedure
    c. code of ethics
    d. social policy

13. Which of the following monitors, measures, and appraises all aspects of an organization's social responsibility performance? (p. 61)
    a. a social procedure
    b. a code of ethics
    c. a social audit
    d. a social policy

14. Areas of social responsibility measurement include all but which of the following? (p. 61)
    a. Economic function area
    b. Quality-of-life area
    c. Gender area
    d. Social investment

15. A social audit does which of the following? (p. 61)
    a. Monitors
    b. Measures
    c. Appraises
    d. All are correct

16. According to one business CEO, who has responsibilities to business to set guidelines? (p. 62)
    a. Government
    b. Society
    c. Individuals
    d. None are correct

Chapter Three – Corporate Social Responsibility and Business Ethics

17. _____ are our concern for good behavior, our obligation to consider not only our own personal well-being but also that of other human beings. (p. 63)
    a. Morals
    b. Values
    c. Ethics
    d. Folklores

18. A(n) _____ is a formal statement that acts as a guide for making decisions and acting within an organization. (p. 64)
    a. stakeholder
    b. social audit
    c. code of ethics
    d. vision statement

19. What is defined as "act the way you would expect others to act toward you?" (p. 66)
    a. Utilitarian principle
    b. Golden rule
    c. Legal test
    d. Four-way test

20. Which of the following standards emphasizes the following: "act in a way that results in the greatest good for the greatest number of people?" (p. 66)
    a. the golden rule
    b. the utilitarian principle
    c. Kant's categorical imperative
    d. the professional ethic

21. "Act in such as way that the action taken under the circumstances could be a universal law, or rule, or behavior" describes which of the following standards? (p. 66)
    a. the golden rule
    b. the utilitarian principle
    c. Kant's categorical imperative
    d. the professional ethic

22. Which of the following standards recommends that managers "take actions that would be viewed as proper by a disinterested panel of professional peers?" (p. 67)
    a. the golden rule
    b. the utilitarian principle
    c. Kant's categorical imperative
    d. the professional ethic

23. The _____ indicates that managers should always ask, "Would I feel comfortable explaining to a national TV audience why I took this action?" (p. 67)
    a. professional ethic test
    b. TV test
    c. legal test
    d. four-way test

Chapter Three – Corporate Social Responsibility and Business Ethics

24. Which of the following standards inquires whether or not the proposed action or decision is legal? (p. 67)
    a. professional ethic test
    b. TV test
    c. legal test
    d. four-way test

25. Using the _____, managers can feel confident that a decision is ethical if they can answer "yes" to the following questions: "Is the decision truthful? Is it fair to all concerned? Will it build goodwill and better friendships? Will it be beneficial to all concerned?" (p. 67)
    a. professional ethic test
    b. TV test
    c. legal test
    d. four-way test

Fill-In

1. _____ is the obligation of management to take action that protects and improves the welfare of society in conjunction with the interests of the organization. (p. 49)

2. Adherence to legislated social responsibilities is the _____ standard of social responsibility performance that business managers must achieve. (p. 52)

3. The greater the degree of effectiveness and efficiency, the more _____ the organization is said to be. (p. 55)

4. The _____ approach considers business as having primarily economic purposes and confines social responsibility activity mainly to existing legislation. (p. 57)

5. The measurement of _____ deals with the degree to which the organization is investing both money and human resources to solve community social problems. (p. 61)

6. A _____ is the process of measuring the present social responsibility activities of an organization to assess its performance in this area. (p. 61)

7. In business, _____ can be defined as the capacity to reflect on values in the corporate decision-making process, to determine how these values and decisions affect stakeholder groups. (p. 63)

8. The employment of ethical business practices can enhance overall corporate health in three important areas: _____, _____, and _____. (p. 64)

9. Ninety percent of Fortune 500 firms, and almost half of all other firms, have _____. (p. 64)

10. _____ commonly address such issues as conflict of interest, competitors, privacy of information, gift giving, and giving and receiving political contributions or business. (p. 64)

Chapter Three – Corporate Social Responsibility and Business Ethics

Answers

Essay

1. The five propositions include:
   a. Proposition 1: Social responsibility arises from social power—this proposition is derived from the premise that business has a significant amount of influence on, or power over, such critical social issues as minority employment and environmental pollution.
   b. Proposition 2: Business shall operate as a two-way open system, with open receipt of inputs from society and open disclosure of its operations to the public—according to this proposition, business must be willing to listen to what must be done to sustain or improve social welfare.
   c. Proposition 3: The social costs and benefits of an activity, product, or service shall thoroughly calculated and considered in deciding whether to proceed with it—this proposition stresses that technical feasibility and economic profitability are not the only factors that should influence business decision making.
   d. Proposition 4: The social costs related to each activity, product, or service shall be passed on to the consumer—this proposition states that business cannot be expected to completely finance activities that may be socially advantageous but economically disadvantageous.
   e. Proposition 5: Business institutions, as citizens, have the responsibility to become involved in certain social problems that are outside their normal areas of operation.—this last proposition points out that if a business possesses the expertise to solve a social problem with which it may not be directly associated, it should be held responsible for helping society solve that problem.

2. The 3 phases include:
   a. Phase 1 consists of the recognition by top management that the organization has some social obligation. Top management then must formulate and communicate some policy about the acceptance of this obligation to all organization members.
   b. Phase 2 involves staff personnel as well as top management. In this phase, top management gathers information related to meeting the social obligation accepted in Phase 1. Staff personnel are generally involved at this point to give advice on technical matters related to meeting the accepted social obligation.
   c. Phase 3 involves division management in addition to the organization personnel already involved from the first two phases. During this phase, top management strives to obtain the commitment of organization members to live up to the accepted social obligation and attempts to create realistic expectations about the effects of such a commitment on organizational productivity.

3. The four areas of measurement include:
   a. The economic function area—a measurement should be made of whether the organization is performing such activities as producing goods and services that people need, creating jobs for society, paying fair wages, and ensuring worker safety.
   b. The quality-of-life area—the measurement of quality of life should focus on whether the organization is improving or degrading the general quality of life in society.
   c. The social investment area—the measurement of social investment deals with the degree to which the organization is investing both money and human resources to solve community social problems.
   d. The problem-solving area—the measurement of problem solving should focus on the degree to which the organization deals with social problems, such as participating in long-range community planning and conducting studies to pinpoint social problems.

Chapter Three – Corporate Social Responsibility and Business Ethics

4. The five responsibilities that society has to business, according to Jerry McAfee, include (1) setting rules that are clear and consistent, (2) keeping the rules technically feasible, (3) making sure the rules are economically feasible, (4) making the rules prospective, not retroactive, and (5) making the rules goal-setting, not procedure-prescribing.

5. The seven standards include:
    a. The golden rule—act in a way you would expect others to act toward you.
    b. The utilitarian principle—act in a way that results in the greatest good for the greatest number of people.
    c. Kant's categorical imperative—act in such a way that the action taken under the circumstances could be a universal way, or rule, or behavior.
    d. The professional ethic—take actions that would be viewed as proper by a disinterested panel of professional peers.
    e. The TV test—managers should always ask, "Would I feel comfortable explaining to a national TV audience why I took this action?"
    f. The legal test—is the proposed action or decision legal? Established laws are general considered minimum standards for ethics.
    g. The four-way test—managers can feel confident that a decision is ethical if they can answer "yes" to the following questions: Is the decision truthful? Is it fair to all concerned? Will it build goodwill and better friendship? Will it be beneficial to all concerned?

True-False

1. T	3. T	5. T	7. F	9. T
2. T	4. T	6. T	8. F	10. F

Multiple Choice

1. d	6. b	11. a	16. b	21. c
2. d	7. a	12. a	17. c	22. d
3. c	8. c	13. c	18. c	23. b
4. a	9. d	14. c	19. b	24. c
5. a	10. b	15. d	20. b	25. d

Fill-In

1. Social responsibility
2. minimum
3. socially responsive
4. social obligation
5. social investment
6. social audit
7. ethics
8. productivity, stakeholder relations, and government regulation
9. ethical codes
10. Codes of ethics

Modern Management (9th ed.)
Part 2 – Modern Management Challenges
Chapter Four – Management and Diversity

Overview

The chapter will cover the many aspects of diversity including the advantages of having a diverse workforce. It will also cover the challenges of managing a diverse workforce, the strategies needed for promoting diversity, and insights into the role of managers in promoting diversity in the organization.

Chapter Outline

Introductory Case: Advantica Making Great Strides in Building a Diverse Company

I. DEFINING DIVERSITY

    A. **Diversity** is the degree of basic human differences among a given population.

        1. Major areas of diversity are gender, race, ethnicity, religion, social class, physical ability, sexual orientation, and age.

    B. The Social Implications of Diversity

        1. Minority group refers to that group of people in the organization who hold most of the positions that command decision-making power, control of resources and information, and access to system rewards.
        2. Minority group refers to that group of people in the organization who are smaller in number or who possess fewer granted rights and lower status than the majority groups.

II. ADVANTAGES OF DIVERSITY IN ORGANIZATIONS

    A. Gaining and Keeping Market Share

    B. Cost Savings

    C. Increased Productivity and Innovation

    D. Better-Quality Management

III. CHALLENGES THAT MANAGERS FACE IN WORKING WITH DIVERSE POPULATIONS

    A. Changing Demographics

        1. Demographics are statistical characteristics of a population

    B. Ethnocentrism and Other Negative Dynamics

        1. **Ethnocentrism** is the belief that one's own group, culture, country, or customs are superior to others.
        2. A prejudice is a preconceived judgment, opinion, or assumption about an issue, behavior, individual, or group of people.
        3. A stereotype is a positive or negative assessment of members of a group or their perceived attributes.

Chapter Four – Management and Diversity

4. Discrimination is the act of treating an issue, person, or behavior unjustly or inequitably on the basis of stereotypes or prejudices.
5. Tokenism refers to being one of very few members of a group in an organization.

C. Negative Dynamics and Specific Groups

1. Women

   a. Gender-role stereotypes are perceptions about the sexes based on what society believes are appropriate behaviors for men and women.
   b. The *glass ceiling* refers to an invisible "ceiling," or barrier to advancement. This term is also used to describe the experiences of other minorities in organizations.
   c. Sexual harassment is defined as any unwanted sexual language, behavior, or imagery negatively affecting an employee.

2. Minorities

   a. Bicultural stress is stress resulting from having to cope with membership in two cultures simultaneously.
   b. Role conflict is the conflict that results when a person has to fill competing roles because of membership in two cultures.
   c. Role overload refers to having too many expectations to comfortably fulfill.

3. Older Workers

   a. Stereotypes and prejudices

4. Workers with Disabilities

III. STRATEGIES FOR PROMOTING DIVERSITY IN ORGANIZATIONS

A. Hudson Institute's Recommended Strategies

1. Stimulate balanced world growth
2. Accelerate productivity increases in service industries
3. Maintain the dynamism of an aging workforce
4. Reconcile conflicting needs of women, work, and families
5. Fully integrate African American and Hispanic workers into the economy
6. Improve the education and skills of all workers

B. Equal Employment and Affirmative Action

1. Reverse discrimination is the term used to describe inequities affecting members of majority group as an outcome of programs designed to help underrepresented groups.

C. Organizational Commitment to Diversity

1. Ignoring differences
2. Complying with external policies
3. Enforcing external policies
4. Responding inadequately
5. Implementing adequate programs
6. Taking effective action

D. Pluralism is an environment in which cultural, group, and individual differences are acknowledged, accepted, and viewed as significant contributors to the entirety.

1. "Golden Rule" approach
2. Assimilation approach
3. "Righting-the-wrongs" approach
4. Cultural-specific approach
5. Multicultural approach

IV. THE ROLE OF THE MANAGER

A. The roles of planning, organizing, influencing, and controlling

B. Management Development and Diversity Training

1. Basic themes

    a. Behavioral awareness
    b. Acknowledgment of biases and stereotypes
    c. Focus on job performance
    d. Avoidance of assumptions
    e. Modification of policy and procedure manuals

2. Stages in Managing a Diverse Workforce

    a. Understanding and influencing employee responses
    b. Getting top-down support

Chapter Four – Management and Diversity

Test Your Knowledge

Essay

1. List five advantages that often result from having a diverse workforce. (p. 76)

2. Define ethnocentrism and discuss the concepts of prejudice and stereotype. (p. 78)

3. Discuss the concept of the *glass ceiling* in organizations. (p. 80)

4. List and discuss the five major categories into which approaches, or strategies have been classified in order to achieve effective workforce diversity. (p. 86)

5. Discuss the four-stage model, which describes how managers progress in managing a diverse workforce. (p. 89)

True-False

T F 1. Diversity means a degree of basic human differences. (p. 74)

T F 2. An advantage of diversity is gaining and keeping market share. (p. 75)

T F 3. A disadvantage of diversity is cost savings. (p. 75)

T F 4. GE has a course called Leveling Multiculturalism. (p. 77)

T F 5. AT&T is a domestic carrier only. (p. 79)

T F 6. A prejudice is a positive or negative assessment of someone. (p. 78)

T F 7. Women must cope with gender-bound roles. (p. 79)

T F 8. One stress on being a minority is bicultural stress. (p. 80)

T F 9. Unfortunately, women and minorities have no challenges in common. (p. 80)

T F 10. Workforce 2000 recommends maintaining the dynamism of an aging workforce. (p. 81)

Multiple Choice

1. _____ refers to that group of people in the organization who hold most of the positions that command decision-making power, control of resources and information, and access to system rewards. (p. 74)
   a. Token group
   b. Minority group
   c. Majority group
   d. Heterogeneous group

Chapter Four – Management and Diversity

2. Which of the following refers to that group of people in the organization who are smaller in number or who possess fewer granted rights and lower status than the majority groups? (p. 74)
   a. Homogeneous group
   b. Heterogeneous group
   c. Majority group
   d. Minority group

3. _____ is the degree of basic human difference among a given population. (p. 74)
   a. Multiculturalism
   b. Culturalism
   c. Diversity
   d. None is correct

4. What among the following are aspects of diversity? (p. 74)
   a. Age
   b. Sexual orientation
   c. Gender
   d. All are correct

5. Which of the following are seen as advantages of diversity in organizations? (p. 76)
   a. Gaining and keeping market share
   b. Cost savings
   c. Increased productivity
   d. All are correct

6. _____ are statistical characteristics of a population. (p. 77)
   a. Psychographics
   b. Geographics
   c. Demographics
   d. Values and norms

7. A(n) _____ is a preconceived judgment, opinion, or assumption about an issue, behavior, individual, or group of people. (p. 78)
   a. prejudice
   b. value
   c. moral
   d. norm

8. Which of the following is a positive or negative assessment of members of a group or their perceived attributes? (p. 78)
   a. an audit
   b. a policy
   c. a value
   d. a stereotype

9. Which of the following was not one of the projects of the Report 2000? (p. 78)
    a. More women will enter the workforce.
    b. The workforce will grow at a greater rate than at any time since the 1930s.
    c. The average age of the workforce will rise.
    d. Immigrants will represent the largest share of increase in both the general population and the workforce.

10. _____ is the belief that one's own group is superior to others. (p. 78)
    a. Tokenism
    b. Stereotyping
    c. Prejudice
    d. Ethnocentrism

11. _____ is the act of treating an issue, person, or behavior unjustly or inequitably on the basis of stereotypes or prejudices. (p. 79)
    a. Discrimination
    b. Pluralism
    c. Multiculturalism
    d. Heterogeneity

12. If you are one of only a few like you in the organization, you are likely to be labeled what? (p. 79)
    a. Odd
    b. Token
    c. Separate but equal
    d. None are correct

13. _____ stereotypes are perceptions about the sexes based on what society believes are appropriate behaviors for men and women. (p. 79)
    a. Heterogeneous
    b. Homogeneous
    c. Gender-role
    d. Pluralistic

14. The "glass ceiling" is an invisible barrier to what? (p. 80)
    a. Advancement
    b. Middle management
    c. Technical jobs
    d. None are correct

15. _____ is the conflict that results when a person has to fill competing roles because of membership in two cultures. (p. 80)
    a. Role overload
    b. Role reversal
    c. Role stereotyping
    d. Role conflict

Chapter Four – Management and Diversity

16. Which of the following refers to having too many expectations to comfortably fulfill? (p. 80)
    a. Role overload
    b. Role reversal
    c. Role stereotyping
    d. Role conflict

17. Which among the following are issues for minorities? (p. 80)
    a. Bicultural stress
    b. Role conflict
    c. Role overload
    d. All are correct

18. What is described as the term used to describe inequities affecting members of the majority group in trying to help the underrepresented? (p. 83)
    a. Positive discrimination
    b. Reverse discrimination
    c. Negative discrimination
    d. Blatant discrimination

19. Which among the following is NOT an approach to pluralism? (p. 86)
    a. Golden rule
    b. Assimilation
    c. Cultural-specific
    d. Just-fair-right

20. _____ is an environment in which cultural, group, and individual differences are acknowledged, accepted, and viewed as significant contributors to the entirety. (p. 86)
    a. Pluralism
    b. Ethnocentrism
    c. Discrimination
    d. Stereotyping

21. Which of the following approaches to diversity relies on the biblical dictate, "Do unto others as you would have them do unto you?" (p. 86)
    a. "Golden Rule" approach
    b. Assimilation approach
    c. "Righting-the-Wrongs" approach
    d. Culture-specific approach

22. The _____ advocates shaping organization members to fit the existing culture of the organization. (p. 86)
    a. "Golden Rule" approach
    b. Assimilation approach
    c. "Righting-the-Wrongs" approach
    d. Culture-specific approach

Chapter Four – Management and Diversity

23. Which of the following approaches to diversity addresses past injustices experienced by a particular group? (p. 86)
    a. "Golden Rule" approach
    b. Assimilation approach
    c. "Righting-the-Wrongs" approach
    d. Culture-specific approach

24. _____ is a learning process designed to raise managers' awareness and develop their competencies to deal with the issues endemic to managing a diverse workforce. (p. 88)
    a. Stereotyping
    b. Tokenism
    c. Ethnocentrism
    d. Diversity training

25. _____ is the process of developing qualities in human resources. (p. 89)
    a. Training
    b. Controlling
    c. Planning
    d. Leading

Fill-In

1. Two related dynamics to ethnocentrism are _____ and _____. (p. 78)

2. _____ occurs when stereotypes are acted upon in ways that affect hiring, pay, or promotion practices. (p. 79)

3. A serious form of discrimination affecting women in organization has been dubbed the _____. (p. 80)

4. _____ is defined as any unwanted sexual language, behavior, or imagery negatively affecting an employee. (p. 80)

5. _____ in one's culture of origin can lead to misunderstandings in the workplace. (p. 80)

6. According to the text, the key to economic growth and competitiveness is _____. (p. 82)

7. _____ refers to the relative worth society places on different ways of existence and functions. (p. 82)

8. The _____ is the federal agency that enforces the laws regulating recruiting and other management practices. (p. 83)

9. The _____ approach teaches employees the norms and practices of another culture to prepare them to interact with people from that culture effectively. (p. 86)

10. The _____ approach gives employees the opportunity to develop an appreciation for both differences of culture and variations in personal characteristics. (p. 87)

Chapter Four – Management and Diversity

Answers

Essay

1. <u>The following are advantages that often result from having a diverse workforce:</u>
    a. Improved ability to gain and keep market share
    b. Cost savings
    c. Increased productivity
    d. A more innovative workforce
    e. Minority and women employees who are more motivated
    f. Better quality of managers
    g. Employees who have internalized the message that "different" does not mean "less than"
    h. Employees who are accustomed to making use of differing worldviews, learning styles, and approaches in the decision-making process and in the cultivation of new ideas
    i. Employees who have developed multicultural competencies
    j. A workforce that is more resilient when faced with change

2. Ethnocentrism is the belief that one's own group, culture, country, or customs are superior to others. Our natural tendency is to judge other groups less favorably than our own. A prejudice is a preconceived judgment, opinion, or assumption about an issue, behavior, or group of people. Stereotype is a positive or negative assessment of members of a group or their perceived attributes.

3. A serious form of discrimination affecting women in organizations has been dubbed the *glass ceiling*. The glass ceiling refers to an invisible "ceiling," or barrier to advancement. This term, originally coined to describe the limits confronting women, is also used to describe the experiences of other minorities in organizations.

4. <u>The five major categories include:</u>
    a. "Golden Rule" approach – this approach to diversity relies on the biblical dictate, "Do unto others as you would have them do unto you."
    b. Assimilation approach – this approach advocates shaping organization members to fit the existing culture of the organization.
    c. "Righting-the-Wrongs" approach – this is an approach that addresses past injustices experienced by a particular group.
    d. "Culture-specific approach – this approach teaches employees the norms and practices of another culture to prepare them to interact with people from that culture effectively.
    e. Multicultural approach – this approach gives employees the opportunity to develop an application for both differences of culture and variations in personal characteristics.

5. In the first stage, known as "unconscious incompetence," managers are unaware of behaviors they engage in that are problematic for members of other groups. In the second stage, "conscious incompetence," managers go through a learning process in which they become conscious of behaviors that make them incompetent in their interactions with members of diverse groups. The third stage is one of becoming "consciously competent": Managers learn how to interact with diverse groups and cultures by deliberately thinking about how to behave. In the last stage, "unconscious competence," managers have internalized these new behaviors and feel so comfortable relating to others different from themselves that they need to devote little conscious effort to doing so.

True-False

1. T
2. T
3. F
4. F
5. F
6. F
7. T
8. T
9. F
10. T

Multiple Choice

1. c
2. d
3. c
4. d
5. d
6. c
7. a
8. d
9. b
10. d
11. a
12. b
13. c
14. a
15. d
16. a
17. d
18. b
19. d
20. a
21. a
22. b
23. c
24. d
25. a

Fill-In

1. prejudices and stereotypes
2. Discrimination
3. *glass ceiling*
4. Sexual harassment
5. Socialization
6. human capital
7. social values
8. Equal Employment Opportunity Commission
9. culture-specific
10. multicultural

Modern Management (9th ed.)
Part 2 – Modern Management Challenges
Chapter Five – Managing in the Global Arena

Overview

An understanding of international management is necessary to be effective and competitive in the fast changing global environment. Issues that must also be studied are the types of international corporations, the risks involved in investing, knowledge concerning who works in these corporations, and insights into managing in a global setting.

Chapter Outline

Introductory Case: Wal-Mart Goes to Japan

I. MANAGING ACROSS THE GLOBE: WHY

There are great opportunities in the international marketplace. There are also great risks and problems in our ever-changing and evolving world economy. Companies enter the global arena at their own risk.

II. FUNDAMENTALS OF INTERNATIONAL MANAGEMENT

International management is defined as the performance of management activities across national borders. Globalization is another name for international management. There are great opportunities for investment as well as risks.

III. CATEGORIZING ORGANIZATIONS BY INTERNATIONAL INVOLVEMENT

There are four levels of international involvement along a continuum.

   A. **Domestic organization** - a company that essentially operates within a single country.

   B. **International organization** - a company that is primarily based within a single country but has continuing, meaningful transactions in other countries.

   C. **Multinational corporation (MNC)** - a company that has significant operations in more than one country.

   D. **Transnational corporation** - a company at the farthest end of the continuum that not only does business in many countries but also uses the management talent in that country to manage the company.

IV. COMPLEXITIES OF MANAGING THE MULTINATIONAL CORPORATION

There are differences in how we manage stateside and in other nations. While this sounds like common sense, Americans have often been accused of just transporting our own management philosophies to other nations without taking their ways into consideration. This usually leads to neither effective relationships nor efficient management. One must always be aware the context one is managing in.

V. RISK AND THE MULTINATIONAL CORPORATION

　　A. Developing a multinational corporation requires a substantial investment in foreign operations.

　　B. Some of the goals of managing foreign investments include:
　　　　1. reducing or eliminating high transportation costs
　　　　2. allowing participation in the rapid expansion of a market abroad
　　　　3. providing foreign technical, design, and marketing skills
　　　　4. earning higher profits

　　C. **Parent company** – the company investing in international operations

　　D. **Host county** – the country in which an investment is made by a foreign company

VI. TYPES OF ORGANIZATION MEMBERS FOUND IN MULTINATIONAL CORPORATIONS

　　A. Organizations that operate in the global businessplace often employ three types of workers:
　　　　1. **Expatriates** – organization members who live and work in a county where they do not have citizenship
　　　　2. **Host-country nationals** – organization members who are citizens of the country in which the facility of a foreign-based organization is located
　　　　3. **Third-country nationals** – organization members who are citizens of one country and who work in another country for an organization headquartered in still another country.

　　B. There are workforce adjustments needed when working in a multinational corporation such as adjusting to a new culture and repatriation.

VII. MANAGEMENT FUNCTIONS AND MULTINATIONAL CORPORATIONS

The primary difference between planning in multinational and domestic organizations is in the plans' components.

　　A. Components of international plans
　　　　1. **Imports/Exports**
　　　　　　a. Importing is buying goods or services from another country.
　　　　　　b. Exporting is selling goods or services to another country.
　　　　2. **License agreement** - a right granted by one company to another to use its brand name, technology, product specifications, and so on in the manufacture or sale of goods and services.
　　　　3. **Direct investing** - using the assets of one company to purchase the operating assets of another company.
　　　　4. **International joint ventures** - partnerships formed by a company in one country with a company in another country for the purpose of pursuing some mutually desirable business undertaking.

VIII. PLANNING AND INTERNATIONAL MARKET AGREEMENTS IN MULTINATIONAL CORPORATIONS

- A. An international market agreement is an arrangement among a cluster of countries that facilitates a high level of trade among these countries.

- B. The European Community (EC) is an international market agreement first formed in 1958 and dedicated to facilitating trade among member nations.

- C. North American Free Trade Agreement (NAFTA) is an international market agreement aimed at facilitating trade among member nations that currently includes the U.S., Mexico, and Canada. Other countries in Central and Latin America are hoping to join.

- D. The Evolving Pacific Rim area is commonly believed to be interested in developing an international market agreement among them that is as effective as the EC has proved to be in Europe.

IX. ORGANIZING MULTINATIONAL CORPORATIONS

- A. The relevant topics of this subject are organizational structure and the selection of managers.

- B. Other key issues are: managerial attitudes toward foreign operations; advantages and disadvantages of each management attitudes

    1. **Ethnocentric attitude** – reflects the belief that multinational corporations should regard home-country management practices as superior to foreign-country management practices.
    2. **Polycentric attitude** – reflects the belief that because foreign managers are closer to foreign organizational units, foreign management practices should generally be viewed as more insightful than home-country management practices.
    3. **Geocentric attitude** – reflects the belief that the overall quality of management recommendations, rather than the location of managers, should determine the acceptability of management practices used to guide multinational corporations.

X. INFLUENCING PEOPLE IN MULTINATIONAL CORPORATIONS

Influencing people in a multinational corporation is more complex and challenging than in a domestic organization.

- A. **Culture** – the set of characteristics of a given group of people and their environment

- B. To successfully influence employees, managers in multinational corporations should:
    1. Acquire a working knowledge of the languages used in countries that house foreign operations
    2. Understand the attitudes of people in countries that house foreign operations
    3. Understand the needs that motivate people in countries housing foreign operations

XI. CONTROLLING MULTINATIONAL CORPORATIONS

There are many complexities to managing an MNC as well as communication issues.

Chapter Five – Managing in the Global Arena

XII. TRANSNATIONAL ORGANIZATIONS

Transnational organizations, also called global organizations, take the entire world as their business area.

XVI. INTERNATIONAL MANAGEMENT: SPECIAL ISSUES

    A.   Maintaining Ethics in International Management

Ethics is also an important concern with international management, such as respecting core human rights, respecting local traditions, and determining right from wrong by examining the context. An understanding of other people's approach to ethics is critical to being successful in any nation.

    B.   Preparing Expatriates for Foreign Assignments
        1. Companies need to assist their employees in adjusting to the new country.
        2. Core elements of an expatriate program include:
           a. Culture profiles
           b. Cultural adaptation
           c. Logistical information
           d. Application

Test Your Knowledge

Essay

1. Discuss the differences between a domestic organization and an international organization. (p. 100)

2. List and discuss the three basic types of workers in multinational organizations. (p. 106)

3. List and discuss the three basic managerial attitudes toward the operation of multinational corporations. (p. 110)

4. Discuss the three steps that managers in multinational corporations should follow to successfully influence employees. (p. 112)

5. Describe the characteristics of the transnational organization. (p. 113)

True-False

T F   1. International management is the performance of management activities across national borders. (p. 98)

T F   2. Global expansion is very slow at this point in time. (p. 98)

T F   3. U.S. investment in foreign nations is expected to slow markedly, but world crises—such as those in Russia and China—continue. (p. 99)

T F   4. High involvement in international markets is called transnational. (p. 101)

T F   5. MNC stands for Multiple National Companies. (p. 101)

Chapter Five – Managing in the Global Arena

T F 6. The parent company is the company investing in the international operations. (p. 105)

T F 7. The parent country is the country in which an investment is made by a foreign company. (p. 105)

T F 8. Exporting is buying goods or services from another country. (p. 108)

T F 9. The European Community is an example of an international market agreement. (p. 109)

T F 10. NAFTA is between Mexico and the U.S. only. (p. 109)

Multiple Choice

1. What is the performance of management activities across national borders? (p. 98)
   a. National management
   b. Planning
   c. International management
   d. Polycentric management

2. Which of the following statements is the most accurate? (p. 99)
   a. The U.S. is likely to slow developing business with other nations.
   b. In the future, business between our country and other countries is likely to accelerate.
   c. Because of world instability, no new development will be happening.
   d. None are correct

3. A(n) _____ organization is a company primarily based within a single country but having continuing, meaningful transactions in other countries. (p. 100)
   a. domestic
   b. international
   c. multinational
   d. transnational

4. On the continuum of international involvement, what is the 3rd level? (p. 100)
   a. Domestic
   b. International
   c. Multinational
   d. Transnational

5. An international organization is primarily based in ____ country. (p. 100)
   a. one
   b. two
   c. three
   d. four

6. A(n) _____ corporation is a company that has significant operations in more than one country. (p. 101)
   a. domestic
   b. international
   c. virtual
   d. multinational

Chapter Five – Managing in the Global Arena

7. Which of the following is the company investing in international operations? (p. 105)
   a. parent company
   b. host company
   c. third company
   d. transmodal company

8. The ____ country is the country in which an investment is made by a foreign company. (p. 105)
   a. parent
   b. grandparent
   c. host
   d. None is correct

9. Which of the following is NOT one of the three basic types of workers in multinational organizations? (p. 106)
   a. transpatriates
   b. expatriates
   c. host-country nationals
   d. third-country nationals

10. _____ is the process of bringing individuals who have been working abroad back to their home country and reintegrating them into the organization's home-country operations. (p. 106)
    a. Expatriation
    b. Internationalization
    c. Repatriation
    d. Globalization

11. All of the following components are commonly included in international plans EXCEPT: (p. 107)
    a. cost efficiencies
    b. license agreements
    c. direct investing
    d. joint ventures

12. _____ is buying goods or services from another country. (p. 108)
    a. Importing
    b. Exporting
    c. Licensing
    d. Franchising

13. Selling goods or services to another country is called _____. (p. 108)
    a. importing
    b. exporting
    c. licensing
    d. franchising

14. A(n) _____ agreement is a right granted by one company to another to use its brand name, technology, and product specifications in the manufacture or sale of goods and services. (p. 108)
    a. importing
    b. exporting
    c. licensing
    d. direct investing

15. _____ is using the assets of one company to purchase the operating assets of another company. (p. 108)
    a. Importing
    b. Exporting
    c. Licensing
    d. Direct investing

16. Investments in foreign lands are expected to accomplish what? (p. 108)
    a. Reduce transportation costs
    b. Allow participation in rapid expansion
    c. Earn higher profits
    d. All are correct

17. A(n) _____ is a partnership formed by a company in one country with a company in another country for the purpose of pursuing some mutually desirable business undertaking. (p. 108)
    a. license agreement
    b. franchise
    c. international joint venture
    d. domestic joint venture

18. An arrangement among a cluster of countries that facilitates a high level of trade among these countries is called a(n) _____. (p. 109)
    a. domestic market agreement.
    b. cross-cultural agreement.
    c. international market agreement.
    d. joint venture.

19. Which of the following countries is NOT a member of the NAFTA? (p. 109)
    a. Mexico
    b. United States
    c. Canada
    d. Germany

20. What does NAFTA stand for? (p. 109)
    a. North African Federation of Territories Associations
    b. North Asian Federation of Trade Associations
    c. North American Free Trade Agreement
    d. None are correct

Chapter Five – Managing in the Global Arena

21. The _____ attitude reflects the belief that multinational corporations should regard home-country management practices as superior to foreign-country management practices. (p. 110)
    a. ethnocentric
    b. polycentric
    c. geocentric
    d. transcentric

22. Which of the following attitudes reflects the belief that foreign management practices should generally be viewed as more insightful than home-country management practices? (p. 110)
    a. ethnocentric attitude
    b. polycentric attitude
    c. geocentric attitude
    d. transcentric attitude

23. The _____ attitude reflects the belief that the overall quality of management recommendations, rather than the location of managers, should determine the acceptability of management practices used to guide multinational corporations. (p. 110)
    a. ethnocentric
    b. polycentric
    c. geocentric
    d. transcentric

24. Which of the following attitudes is considered most appropriate for long-term organizational success? (p. 110)
    a. ethnocentric attitude
    b. polycentric attitude
    c. geocentric attitude
    d. transcentric attitude

25. According to the text, _____ are also called global organizations. (p. 113)
    a. domestic organizations
    b. international organizations
    c. multinational organizations
    d. transnational organizations

Fill-In

1. The _____ represents the third level of international involvement. (p. 100)

2. Organization members who live and work in a country where they do not have citizenship are referred to as _____. (p. 106)

3. _____ are organization members who are citizens of the country in which the facility of a foreign-based organization is located. (p. 106)

4. Organization members who are citizens of one country and who work in another country for an organization headquartered in still another country are referred to as _____. (p. 106)

5. _____ is the process of bringing individuals who have been working (p. 106) abroad back to their home country and reintegrating them into the organization's home-country operations.

6. A(n) _____ is a right granted by one company to another to use its (p. 108) brand name, technology, product specifications, in the manufacture or sale of goods or services.

7. Joint ventures between _____ are becoming more and more common (p. 108) as companies strive for greater economies of scale and higher standards in product quality and delivery.

8. Managers with a(n) _____ attitude are prone to stereotype home-country (p. 110) management practices as sound and reasonable and foreign management practices as faulty and unreasonable.

9. _____ is the set of characteristics of a given group of people and their (p. 112) environment.

10. _____ organizations take the entire world as their business arena. (p. 113)

Answers

Essay

1. Domestic and international organizations
   a. **Domestic organizations** are organizations that essentially operate within a single country. These organizations normally not only acquire necessary resources within a single country but also sell their goods or services within that same county. Although this category is not determined by size, most domestic organizations today are quite small.
   b. **International organizations** are organizations that are primarily based within a single country but have continuing, meaningful international transactions—such as making sales and/or purchases of materials—in other countries. International organizations are more extensively involved in the international arena than are domestic organization, but less so than either multinational or transnational organizations.

2. Three basic types of workers in multinational organizations:
   a. Expatriates—organization members who are citizens of the country in which the facility of a foreign-based organization is located
   b. Host-country nationals—organization members who are citizens of the country in which the facility of a foreign-based organization is located
   c. Third-county nationals—organization members who are citizens of one country and who work in another country for an organization headquartered in still another country

3. Three basic managerial attitudes toward the operation of multinational corporations:
   a. The **ethnocentric attitude** reflects the belief that multinational corporations should regard home-country management practices as superior to foreign-country management practices. Managers with an ethnocentric attitude are prone to stereotype home-country management practices as sound and reasonable and foreign management practices as faulty and unreasonable.
   b. The **polycentric attitude** reflects the belief that because foreign managers are closer to foreign organizational units, they probably understand them better, and therefore foreign management

Chapter Five – Managing in the Global Arena

practices should be generally viewed as more insightful than home-country management practices.

c. The **geocentric attitude** reflects the belief that the overall quality of management recommendations, rather than the location of managers, should determine the acceptability of management practices used to guide multinational corporations. The geocentric attitude is considered most appropriate for long-term organizational success.

4. <u>Three steps that managers in MNCs should follow to successfully influence employees:</u>
   a. Acquire a working knowledge of the languages used in countries that house foreign operations—multinational managers attempting to operate without such knowledge are prone to making costly mistakes.
   b. Understand the attitudes of people in countries that house foreign operations—an understanding of these attitudes can help managers design business practices that are suitable for unique foreign situations.
   c. Understand the needs that motivate people in countries housing foreign operations—managers in multinational corporations must present employees in different countries with the opportunity to satisfy personal needs while being productive within the organization.

5. **Transnational organizations**, also called global organizations, take the entire world as their business arena. Doing business where it makes sense is primary; national borders are considered inconsequential. The transnational organization transcends any single home country, with ownership, control, and management being from many different countries. Transnational organizations represent the fourth, and maximum, level of international activity.

True/False

1. T	3. T	5. F	7. F	9. T
2. F	4. T	6. T	8. F	10. F

Multiple Choice

1. c	6. d	11. a	16. d	21. a
2. b	7. a	12. a	17. c	22. b
3. a	8. c	13. b	18. c	23. c
4. c	9. a	14. c	19. d	24. c
5. a	10. c	15. d	20. c	25. d

Fill-In

1. multinational organization
2. expatriates
3. Host-country nationals
4. third-country nationals
5. repatriation
6. license agreement
7. car manufacturers
8. ethnocentric
9. Culture
10. Transnational

Modern Management (9th ed.)
Part 3 - Planning
Chapter Six – Principles of Planning

Overview

This chapter will cover the definition of planning as well as present the purposes of planning. It will outline knowledge of the advantages and potential disadvantages of planning. In addition, it will explain the major steps in the planning process including the subsystems, how the CEO relates to the process, the role of planners, and guidelines on how to get the greatest return from the planning process.

Chapter Outline

Introductory Case: American Airlines Planning to Make the Internet Work

I. GENERAL CHARACTERISTICS OF PLANNING

   A. Defining Planning

   Planning is the process of determining how the management system will achieve its objectives. In other words, it determines how the organization can get where it wants to go.

   B. Purposes of Planning

   There are many reasons for planning. Given among the most important are the two purposes of protective and affirmative. Another reason is "to facilitate the accomplishment of enterprise and objectives."

   C. Planning: Advantages and Disadvantages

   Planning has many benefits: future-orientation; enhances decision coordination; emphasizes organizational objectives. Overall, planning is an advantage to the organization. Inadequate planning can lead to failure; it can be overemphasized, taking too much managerial time. However, advantages tend to outweigh disadvantages.

   D. Primacy of Planning

   Planning is primary management function, the one that precedes and is the basis for organizing, influencing and controlling functions of managers.

II. STEPS IN THE PLANNING PROCESS

   A. The planning process consists of the following six steps:
   1. State organizational objectives
   2. List alternative ways of reaching objectives
   3. Develop premises on which to base each alternative
   4. Choose the best alternative for reaching objectives
   5. Develop plans to pursue the chosen alternative
   6. Put the plans into action

III. THE PLANNING SUBSYSTEM

A subsystem is a system created as part of the process of the overall management system. The elements include input, process and output.

IV. ORGANIZATIONAL OBJECTIVES: PLANNING'S FOUNDATION

A. Definition of organizational objectives
1. **Organizational objectives** – the targets toward which the open management system is directed. They flow from the organization's purpose or mission.
2. **Organizational purpose** – what the organization exists to do, given a particular group of customers and customer needs.

B. Three points that summarize organizational business objectives
1. Profit is the motivating force for managers
2. Service to customers by the provision of desired economic values justifies the existence of the business
3. Managers have social responsibilities in accordance with the ethical and moral codes of the society in which the business operates

V. AREAS FOR ORGANIZATIONAL OBJECTIVES

A. Eight key areas in which managers should set management system objectives
1. Market standing – management should set objectives indicating where it would like to be in relation to its competitors
2. Management should set objectives outlining its commitment to the development of new methods of operation
3. Management should set objectives outlining the target levels of production
4. Physical and financial resources – management should set objectives regarding the use, acquisition, and maintenance of capital and monetary resources
5. Profitability – management should set objectives that specify the profit the company would like to generate
6. Managerial performance and development – management should set objectives that specify rates and levels of managerial productivity and growth
7. Worker performance and attitude – management should set objectives that specify rates of worker productivity as well as desirable attitudes for workers to process
8. Public responsibility – management should set objectives that indicate the company's responsibilities to its customers and society and the extent to which the company intends to live up to those responsibilities

VI. WORKING ORGANIZATIONAL OBJECTIVES

A. In general, an organization should set three types of objectives.
1. **Short-term objectives** – targets to be achieved in one year or less
2. **Intermediate-term objectives** – targets to be achieved in one to five years
3. **Long-term objectives** – targets to be achieved in five to seven years

B. **Principle of the objective** – a management guideline that recommends that before managers indicate any action, they should clearly determine, understand, and state organizational objectives

C. **Hierarchy of objectives** – the overall organizational objectives and the subobjectives assigned to the various people or units of the organization

D. **Suboptimization** – a condition wherein organizational subobjectives are conflicting or not directly aimed at accomplishing the overall organizational objectives.

E. Guidelines for Establishing Quality Objectives
1. Let the people responsible for attaining the objectives have a voice in setting them
2. State objectives as specifically as possible
3. Relate objectives to specific actions whenever necessary
4. Pinpoint expected results
5. Set goals high enough that employees will have to strive to meet them, but not so high that employees give up trying to meet them
6. Specify when goals are expected to be achieved
7. Set objectives only in relation to other organizational objectives
8. State objectives clearly and simply

VII. MANAGEMENT BY OBJECTIVES (MBO)

A. Management by objectives – a management approach that uses organizational objectives as the primary means of managing organizations

B. Three basic parts of an MBO strategy
1. All individuals within an organization are assigned a specialized set of objectives that they try to reach during a normal operating period
2. Performance reviews are conducted periodically to determine how close individuals are to attaining their objectives
3. Rewards are given to individuals on the basis of how close they come to reaching their goals

C. The MBO process consists of five steps
1. Review organizational objectives
2. Set worker objectives
3. Monitor progress
4. Evaluate performance
5. Give rewards

VIII. PLANNING AND THE CHIEF EXECUTIVE

A. Final Responsibility

1. The CEO has final responsibility for organizational planning.
2. As planners, chief executives seek answers to the following broad questions
   a. In what direction should the organization be going?
   b. In what direction is the organization going now?
   c. Should something be done to change this direction?
   d. Is the organization continuing in an appropriate direction?

Chapter Six – Principles of Planning

B. Planning Assistance

The planner is probably the most important input in the planning subsystem.

C. Qualifications of Planners

1. Planners should have four basic qualifications
   a. They should have considerable practical experience within their organization
   b. They should be capable of replacing any narrow view of the organization they may have acquired while holding other organizational positions
   c. They should have some knowledge of and interest in the social, political, technical, and economic trends that could affect the future of the organization
   d. They should be able to work well with others

D. Evaluation of Planners
   1. Like everyone else in the organization, planners need to be evaluated as to their contribution to the organization.
   2. The following objective criteria would suggest that a planner is doing a reputable job:
      a. Organizational plan is in writing
      b. Plan is the result of all elements o the management team working together
      c. Plan defines present and possible future business of the organization
      d. Plan specifically mentions organizational objectives
      e. Plan identifies future opportunities and suggests how to take advantage of them
      f. Plan emphasizes both internal and external environment
      g. Plan describes the attainment of objectives in operational terms whenever possible
      h. Plan includes both long- and short-term recommendations

Test Your Knowledge

Essay

1. List and discuss the six steps in the planning process. (p. 126)
2. List and discuss the five of the eight key areas in which Peter Drucker advised managers to set management system objectives. (p. 130)
3. List and discuss five general guidelines that managers can use to increase the quality of their objectives. (p. 133)
4. Define the management by objectives (MBO) approach and list and discuss the five steps involved in the MBO process. (p. 134)
5. Describe the four primary qualifications that planners should have. (p. 137)

True-False

T F 1. Planning is the second most important management function with influencing first. (p. 125)

T F 2. Planning is used to determine how the organization can get where it wants to go. (p. 125)

T F 3. One of the advantages of planning is that it emphasizes the past. (p. 125)

52

Chapter Six – Principles of Planning

T   F   4. The first step in the planning process is to develop premises.   (p. 126)

T   F   5. A subsystem is a system created as part of the process of the overall   (p. 127)
            management system.

T   F   6. The fundamental purpose of planning is to assist the organization in   (p. 125)
            reaching goals.

T   F   7. The final responsibility for planning lies with top management.   (p. 135)

T   F   8. The planners have the final responsibility for all plans.   (p. 135)

T   F   9. The planner is probably the most important input into the planning subsystem.   (p. 137)

T   F   10. Planners need to have practical experience within their organization.   (p. 137)

Multiple Choice

1. Which of the following best describes planning?   (p. 124)
    a. Process
    b. Done once a year
    c. Only done by top-management
    d. None are correct

2. What is the fundamental purpose of planning?   (p. 125)
    a. Assist organization in hiring
    b. Assist organization in finances
    c. Assist organization in reaching goals
    d. None are correct

3. Advantages of planning are all but which of the following?   (p. 125)
    a. Future-oriented
    b. Helps decision coordination
    c. Emphasizes organizational objectives
    d. Makes decisions

4. Which of the following are steps in the planning process?   (p. 126)
    a. state organizational objectives
    b. list alternatives
    c. develop premise
    d. all are correct

5. _____ are the assumptions on which an alternative to reaching an   (p. 126)
    organizational objective is based.
    a. premises
    b. policies
    c. procedures
    d. visions

53

Chapter Six – Principles of Planning

6. A _____ is a system created as part of the process of the overall management system.. (p. 127)
    a. system
    b. underground system
    c. subsystem
    d. None are correct

7. _____ are the targets toward which the open management system is directed. (p. 128)
    a. Organizational objectives
    b. Organizational procedures
    c. Organizational policies
    d. Organizational plans

8. Which of the following flows from the organization's purpose or mission? (p. 128)
    a. organizational procedures
    b. organizational policies
    c. organizational objectives
    d. organizational plans

9. The _____ is what the organization exists to do, given a particular group of customers and customer needs. (p. 128)
    a. organizational culture
    b. organizational purpose
    c. organizational plan
    d. organizational hierarchy

10. Which of the following areas for organizational objectives suggests that management should set objectives indicating where it would like to be in relation to its competitors? (p. 130)
    a. market standing
    b. innovation
    c. productivity
    d. physical and financial resources

11. _____ is the area for organizational objective that suggests that management should set objectives outlining its commitment to the development of new methods of operation. (p. 130)
    a. Market standing
    b. Innovation
    c. Productivity
    d. Physical and financial resources

12. Which of the following areas for organizational objectives suggests that management should set objectives outlining the target levels of production? (p. 130)
    a. market standing
    b. innovation
    c. productivity
    d. physical and financial resources

13. _____ is the area for organizational objectives that suggests that (p. 131)
    management should set objectives regarding the use, acquisition, and maintenance
    of capital and monetary resources.
    a. Market standing
    b. Innovation
    c. Productivity
    d. Physical and financial resources

14. Which of the following areas for organizational objectives suggests that (p. 131)
    management should set objectives that specify the profit the company would like
    to generate?
    a. productivity
    b. profitability
    c. managerial performance and development
    d. public responsibility

15. _____ is the area for organizational objectives that suggests that (p. 131)
    management should set objectives that indicate the company's responsibilities
    to its customers and society.
    a. Productivity
    b. Profitability
    c. Managerial performance and development
    d. Public responsibility

16. Targets to be achieved in one year or less are referred to as _____. (p. 131)
    a. short-term objectives.
    b. intermediate-term objectives.
    c. long-term objectives.
    d. virtual objectives.

17. _____ are targets to be achieved within one to five years. (p. 131)
    a. Short-term objectives
    b. Intermediate-term objectives
    c. Long-term objectives
    d. Virtual objectives

18. Targets to be achieved within five to seven years are referred to as (p. 131)
    _____.
    a. short-term objectives.
    b. intermediate-term objectives.
    c. long-term objectives. (131)
    d. virtual objectives.

19. The _____ is a management guideline that recommends that before (p. 132)
    managers initiate any action, they should clearly determine, understand, and state
    organizational objectives.
    a. hierarchy of objectives
    b. hierarchy of planning
    c. principle of the objective
    d. principle of competitiveness

Chapter Six – Principles of Planning

20. A(n) _____ is the overall organizational objectives and the subobjectives assigned to the various people or units of the organization. (p. 132)
    a. hierarchy of objectives
    b. hierarchy of planning
    c. principle of the objective
    d. principle of competitiveness

21. _____ is a condition wherein organizational subobjectives are conflicting or not directly aimed at accomplishing the overall organizational objectives. (p. 132)
    a. Subcategorization
    b. Suboptimization
    c. Subjectivity
    d. Objectivity

22. The final responsibility for planning lies with _____ management. (p. 135)
    a. middle
    b. planning
    c. top
    d. All of the above

23. What is considered the most important input in the planning subsystem? (p. 137)
    a. The middle managers
    b. The Board of Directors
    c. The planners
    d. None are correct

24. The Quality Spotlight highlights which company? (p. 136)
    a. Sun Microsystems
    b. Apple
    c. IBM
    d. Digital

25. Which of the following is NOT mentioned as one of the four primary qualifications that planners should have? (p. 137)
    a. Planners should have significant theoretical experience within their organization.
    b. Planners should be capable of replacing any narrow view of the organization they may have acquired while holding other organizational positions.
    c. Planners should have some knowledge of and interest in the external forces that affect the organization.
    d. Planners should be able to work well with others.

Fill-In

1. _____ is the process of determining how the management system will achieve its objectives. (p. 124)

2. The _____ function pushes managers to coordinate their decisions. (p. 125)

3. One way to approach implementation is to view planning activities as an organizational subsystem. (p. 127)

Chapter Six – Principles of Planning

4. The primary purpose of business organization is usually to _____. (p. 130)

5. The _____ is a management guideline that recommends that before managers initiate any action, they should clearly determine, understand, and state organizational objectives. (p. 132)

6. The overall organizational objective and the subobjectives assigned to the various people or units of the organization are referred to as a(n) _____. (p. 132)

7. _____ is a condition wherein subobjectives are conflicting or not directly aimed at accomplishing the overall organizational objective.

8. Managers can minimize _____ by developing a thorough understanding of how various parts of the organization relate to one another and by ensuring subobjectives properly reflect these relations. (p. 133)

9. Management by objectives was popularized mainly through the writings of _____. (p. 133)

10. The _____ is probably the most important input in the planning subsystem. (p. 137)

Answers

Essay

1. <u>The six steps in the planning process</u>
   a. **State organizational objectives**—since planning focuses on how the management system will reach organizational objectives, a clear statement of those objectives is necessary before planning can begin.
   b. **List alternative ways of reaching objectives**—once organizational objectives have been clearly stated, a manager should list as many available alternatives as possible for reaching those objectives.
   c. **Develop premises on which to base each alternative**—to a large extent, the feasibility of using any one alternative to reach organizational objectives is determined by the premises, or assumptions, on which the alternative is based.
   d. **Choose the best alternative for reaching objectives**—an evaluation of alternatives must include an evaluation of the premises on which the alternatives are based.
   e. **Develop plans to pursue the chosen alternative**—after an alternative has been chosen, a manager begins to develop strategic and tactical plans.
   f. **Put the plans into action**—once plans that furnish the organization with both long-range and short-range direction have been developed, they must be implemented.

2. <u>Key area in which managers should set management system objectives</u>
   a. **Market standing**—management should set objectives indicating where it would like to be in relation to its competitors.
   b. **Innovation**—management should set objectives outlining its commitment to the development of new methods of operations.
   c. **Productivity**—management should set objectives outlining the target levels of production.
   d. **Physical and financial resources**—management should set objectives regarding the use, acquisition, and maintenance of capital and monetary resources.
   e. **Profitability**—management should set objectives that specify the profit the company would like to generate.

Chapter Six – Principles of Planning

   f. **Managerial performance and development**—management should set objectives that specify rates and levels of managerial productivity and growth.
   g. **Worker performance and attitude**—management should set objectives that specify rates of worker productivity as well as desirable attitudes for workers to possess.
   h. **Public responsibility**—management should set objectives that indicate the company's responsibilities to its customers and society and the extent to which the company intends to live up to those responsibilities.

3. <u>General guidelines that managers can use to increase the quality of their objectives</u>
   a. Let the people responsible for attaining the objectives have a voice in setting them—often the people responsible for attaining the objectives know their job situation better than the managers do and can therefore help to make the objectives more realistic.
   b. State objectives as specific as possible—precise statements minimize confusion and ensure that employees have explicit directions for what they should do.
   c. Related objectives to specific actions whenever necessary—in this way, employees do not have to infer what they should do to accomplish their goals.
   d. Pinpoint expected results—employees should know exactly how managers will determine whether or not an objective has been reached.
   e. Set goals high enough that employees will have to strive to meet them, but not so high that employees give up trying to meet them—managers want employees to work hard but not to become frustrated.
   f. Specify when goals are expected to be achieved—employees must have a time frame for accomplishing their objectives
   g. State objectives clearly and simply—the written or spoken word should not impede communicating a goal to organization members.

4. Management by objectives is a management approach that uses organizational objectives as the primary means of managing organizations. The MBO process consists of five steps:
   a. Review organizational objectives—the manager gains a clear understanding of the organization's overall objectives.
   b. Set worker objectives—the manager and worker meet to agree on worker objectives to be reached by the end of the normal operating period.
   c. Monitor progress—at intervals during the normal operating period, the manager and worker check to see if the objectives are being reached.
   d. Evaluate performance—at the end of the normal operating period, the worker's performance is judged by the extent to which the worker reached the objectives.
   e. Give rewards—rewards given to the worker are based on the extent to which the objectives were reached.

5. <u>Four primary qualifications that planners should have</u>
   a. First, they should have considerable practical experience within their organization. Preferably, they should have been executives in one or more of the organization's major departments.
   b. Second, planners should be capable of replacing any narrow view of the organization they may have acquired while holding other organizational positions with an understanding of the organization as a whole.
   c. Third, planners should have some knowledge of and interest in the social, political, technical, and economic trends that could affect the future of the organization.
   d. The fourth and last qualification for planners is that they be able to work well with others. The ability to communicate clearly, both orally and in writing, is one of most important characteristic of a good planner.

Chapter Six – Principles of Planning

True-False

1. F
2. T
3. F
4. F
5. T
6. T
7. T
8. F
9. T
10. T

Multiple Choice

1. a
2. c
3. d
4. d
5. a
6. c
7. a
8. c
9. b
10. a
11. b
12. c
13. d
14. b
15. d
16. a
17. b
18. c
19. c
20. a
21. b
22. c
23. c
24. a
25. a

Fill-In

1. Planning
2. planning
3. subsystem
4. make a profit
5. principle of the objective
6. hierarchy of objectives
7. Suboptimization
8. suboptimization
9. Peter Drucker
10. planner

Modern Management (9th ed.)
Part 3 - Planning
Chapter Seven – Making Decisions

Overview

Making decisions is at the heart of the manager's job. In the analysis of decision-making, there are programmed and unprogrammed decisions, as well as conditions wherein the decision is made easier because there is complete certainty. In other decision situations, there is great uncertainty caused by any number of variables, known and unknown. Among the various approaches developed to assist managers in making decisions are probability theory and decision trees. Dimensions of group decision-making and the advantages and disadvantages of this decision-making process are also discussed in this chapter.

Chapter Outline

Introductory Case: Gateway Chief Makes Daring Decisions

I. FUNDAMENTALS OF DECISIONS

   A. Definition of a Decision

   Decision - a choice made between two or more available alternatives.

   B. Types of Decisions
      1. **Programmed decisions** – decisions that are routine and repetitive and that typically require specific handling methods
      2. **Nonprogrammed decisions** – typically one-shot decisions that are usually less structured than programmed decisions

   C. The Responsibility for Making Organizational Decisions
      1. **Scope of Decisions** – the proportion of the total management system that a particular decision will affect
      2. **Consensus** – an agreement on a decision by all individuals involved in making that decision

   D. Elements of the Decision Situation

   Decision makers are the individuals or groups that actually make the choice among alternatives. Weak decision makers usually have one of four orientations:

      1. Decision makers who have a **receptive orientation** believe that the source of all good is outside themselves, and therefore they rely heavily on suggestions from other organization members.
      2. Decision makers with an **exploitative orientation** believe that the source of all good is outside themselves, and they are willing to steal ideas as necessary in order to make good decisions.
      3. The **hoarding orientation** is characterized by the desire to preserve the status quo as much as possible. Decision makers with this orientation accept little outside help, isolate themselves from others, and are extremely self-reliant.
      4. **Marketing-oriented** decision makers look upon themselves as commodities that are only as valuable as the decision they make. Thus they try to make decisions that will enhance their value and are highly conscious of what others think of their decisions.

Chapter Seven – Making Decisions

II. THE DECISION-MAKING PROCESS

The decision-making process comprises the steps the decision maker takes to arrive at this choice. In order, the decision-making steps are as follows:

- A. Identifying the Existing Problem
- B. Listing Alternative Solutions
- C. Selecting the Most Beneficial Alternative
- D. Implementing the Chosen Alternative
- E. Gathering Problem-Related Feedback

III. DECISION-MAKING CONDITIONS

In general, there are three different conditions under which decisions are made. Each of these conditions is based on the degree to which the future outcome of a decision alternative is predictable.

- A. **Complete certainty condition** – the decision-making situation in which the decision maker knows exactly what the results of an implemented alternative will be

- B. **Complete uncertainty condition** – the decision-making situation in which the decision maker has only enough information to estimate how probable the outcome of implemented alternatives will be

- C. **Risk condition** – the decision-making situation in which the decision maker has only enough information to estimate how probable the outcome of implemented alternatives will be.

IV. DECISION-MAKING TOOLS

- A. Probability theory and expected value
    1. **Probability theory** – a decision-making tool used in risk situations
    2. **Expected value** – the measurement of the anticipated value of some event, determined by multiplying the income an event would produce by its probability of producing that income

- B. **Decision tree** – a graphic decision-making tool typically used to evaluate decisions involving a series of steps

V. GROUP DECISION-MAKING

- A. Advantages and Disadvantages of Using Groups to Make Decisions

- B. Processes for Making Group Decisions

    1. **Brainstorming** – the group decision-making process in which negative feedback on any suggested alternative to any group member is forbidden until all group members have presented alternatives that they perceive as valuable
    2. **Nominal Group Technique** – a group decision-making process in which every group member is assured of equal participation in making the group decision

Chapter Seven – Making Decisions

3. **The Delphi Technique** – a group decision-making process that involves circulating questionnaires on a specific problem among group members, sharing the questionnaire results with them, and then continuing to recirculate and refine individual responses.
4. Evaluating group decision-making processes

Test Your Knowledge

Essay

1. Compare the differences between programmed decisions and nonprogrammed decisions. Include a specific example to support your answer. (p. 146)

2. List and discuss the four orientations of weak decision makers. (p. 150)

3. List the five steps of the decision-making process. (p. 152)

4. Discuss the characteristics of the following decision-making conditions: (1) complete certainty, (2) complete uncertainty, and (3) risk. (p. 155)

5. List and discuss the three primary processes for making group decisions. (p. 159)

True-False

T F 1. Nonprogrammed decisions are typically simple decisions. (p. 145)

T F 2. A decision is a choice made between at least 3 to 4 alternatives available. (p. 146)

T F 3. Programmed decisions are routine ones. (p. 146)

T F 4. Consensus is agreement on a decision by a majority of those making the decision. (p. 148)

T F 5. Relevant alternatives are seen as the feasible ones. (p. 151)

T F 6. Decision-making is basically a process. (p. 152)

T F 7. The first step in decision-making is to list possible alternatives for solving the problem. (p. 152)

T F 8. Feedback is an important element in the decision process. (p. 154)

T F 9. In a condition of risk, only enough information is available to estimate how probable the outcome of implemented alternatives will be. (p. 155)

T F 10. Probability theory is used under conditions of certainty (p. 156)

Multiple Choice

1. Decision making is a choice between ____ or ____ available alternatives. (p. 146)
   a. 1 or more
   b. 2 or more
   c. 3 or more
   d. 4 or more

Chapter Seven – Making Decisions

2. Nonprogrammed decisions are typically _____ decisions. (p. 145)
   a. repetitive
   b. simple
   c. one-shot
   d. None is correct

3. Programmed decisions are _____ and _____. (p. 146)
   a. routine and simple
   b. routine and complex
   c. routine and repetitive
   d. repetitive and complex

4. The _____ is the proportion of the total management system that a particular decision will affect. (p. 148)
   a. scope of the decision
   b. intensity of the decision
   c. depth of the decision
   d. subjectivity of the decision

5. The broader the scope of the decision, the _____ the level of the manager responsible. (p. 148)
   a. lower
   b. higher
   c. middle
   d. None are correct

6. _____ is an agreement on a decision by all individuals involved in making that decision. (p. 148)
   a. Majority
   b. Consensus
   c. Minority
   d. Hypothesis

7. Which of the following is NOT one of the four orientations of weak decision makers? (p. 150)
   a. projective orientation
   b. receptive orientation
   c. exploitative orientation
   d. hoarding orientation

8. Decision makers who have a(n) _____ orientation believe that the source of all good is outside themselves. (p. 150)
   a. receptive
   b. exploitative
   c. hoarding
   d. marketing-oriented

Chapter Seven – Making Decisions

9. Which of the following types of decision makers are willing to steal ideas as necessary in order to make good decisions? (p. 150)
    a. receptive orientation
    b. exploitative orientation
    c. hoarding orientation
    d. marketing-oriented orientation

10. Decision makers who have a(n) _____ orientation accept little outside help, isolate themselves from others, and are extremely self-reliant. (p. 150)
    a. receptive
    b. exploitative
    c. hoarding
    d. marketing-oriented

11. Which of the following types of decision makers try to make decisions that will enhance their value and are highly conscious of what others think of their decisions? (p. 150)
    a. receptive orientation
    b. exploitative orientation
    c. hoarding orientation
    d. marketing-oriented orientation

12. _____ are considered feasible for solving an existing problem and for implementation. (p. 151)
    a. Relevant alternatives
    b. Bipolar alternatives
    c. Subjective alternatives
    d. Irrelevant alternatives

13. The _____ comprises the steps the decision maker takes to make a decision. (p. 152)
    a. consumer purchase process
    b. decision-making process
    c. goal-setting process
    d. idea screening process

14. Which of the following is the first step in the decision-making process? (p. 152)
    a. list possible alternatives for solving the problem
    b. identify an existing problem
    c. select the most beneficial alternatives
    d. implement the alternatives

15. The decision process is made up of three assumptions. Which one of the following is not one? (p. 152)
    a. Humans are economic beings.
    b. Humans entertain all alternative to a decision.
    c. Humans can rank order values when making a decision.
    d. Humans are not very rational.

Chapter Seven – Making Decisions

16. Which of the following is NOT one of the three different conditions under which decisions are made? (p. 155)
    a. complete certainty
    b. complete uncertainty
    c. risk
    d. all of the selections represent conditions under which decisions are made

17. The _____ condition is the decision-making situation in which the decision maker knows exactly what the results of an implemented alternative will be. (p. 155)
    a. complete certainty
    b. complete uncertainty
    c. subjectivity
    d. risk

18. Which of the following conditions represent the decision-making situation in which the decision maker has absolutely no idea what the results of an implemented alternative will be? (p. 155)
    a. complete certainty
    b. complete uncertainty
    c. subjectivity
    d. risk

19. The _____ condition is the decision-making situation in which the decision maker has only enough information to estimate how probable the outcome of implemented alternatives will be. (p. 155)
    a. complete certainty
    b. complete uncertainty
    c. subjectivity
    d. risk

20. Probability theory is used under what conditions? (p. 156)
    a. Risk
    b. Certainty
    c. Stability
    d. None are correct

21. _____ is the measurement of the anticipated value of some event. (p. 156)
    a. Risk
    b. Expected value
    c. Critical point
    d. Certainty

22. A(n) _____ is a graphic decision-making tool typically used to evaluate decisions involving a series of steps. (p. 157)
    a. perceptual map
    b. decision tree
    c. policy
    d. procedure

65

Chapter Seven – Making Decisions

23. Which of the following is a group decision-making process in which negative feedback on any suggested alternative to any group member is forbidden until all group members have presented alternatives that they perceive as valuable? (p. 159)

    a. brainstorming
    b. idea screening
    c. concept development
    d. test marketing

24. Which of the following is NOT a primary process for making group decisions? (p. 160)
    a. brainstorming
    b. nominal group technique
    c. Delphi technique
    d. all the selections represent primary processes for making group decisions

25. _____ is a group decision-making process in which every group member is assured of equal participation in making the group decision. (p. 160)
    a. Nominal group technique
    b. Delphi technique
    c. Concept technique
    d. Perceptual technique

Fill-In

1. Probably the most generally accepted method of categorizing decisions is based on _____. (p. 146)

2. The broader the scope of a decision, the _____ the level of the manager responsible for making that decision. (p. 148)

3. _____, the first element of the decision situation, are the individuals or groups that actually make the choice among alternatives. (p. 150)

4. _____ is essentially a problem-solving process that involves eliminating barriers to organizational goal attainment. (p. 152)

5. Under conditions of _____, managers have complete knowledge about a decision. (p. 155)

6. The _____ condition would exist if there were no historical data on which to base a decision. (p. 155)

7. The risk condition is a broad one in which _____ of risk can be associated with decisions. (p. 156)

8. _____ refers to the likelihood that an event or outcome will actually occur. (p. 156)

9. _____ is carefully designed to encourage all group members to contribute as many viable decision alternatives as they can think of. (p. 159)

10. The _____ is designed to ensure that each group member has equal participation in making the group decision. (p. 160)

Answers

Essay

1. Programmed vs. nonprogrammed decisions:
   a. Programmed decisions are routine and repetitive, and the organization typically develops specific ways to handle them. A programmed decision might involve determining how products will be arranged on the shelves of a supermarket. For this kind of routine, repetitive problem, standard-arrangement decisions are typically made according to established management guidelines.
   b. Nonprogrammed decisions are typically one-shot decisions that are usually less structured than programmed decisions. An example of the type of nonprogrammed decision that more and more managers are having to make is whether to expand operations in the "forgotten continent" of Africa.

2. Four orientations of weak decision makers:
   a. Decision makers who have a **receptive** orientation believe that the source of all good is outside themselves, and therefore they rely heavily on suggestions from other organization members. Basically, they want others to make their decisions for them.
   b. Decision makers with an **exploitative** orientation also believe that the source of all good is outside themselves, and they are willing to steal ideas as necessary in order to make good decisions. They build their organizations on others' ideas and typically hog all the credit themselves, extending little or none to the originators of the ideas.
   c. The **hoarding** orientation is characterized by the desire to preserve the status quo as much as possible. Decision makers with this orientation little outside help, isolate themselves from others, and are extremely self-reliant. They are obsessed with maintaining their present position and status.
   d. **Marketing**-oriented decision makers look upon themselves as commodities that are only as valuable as the decisions they make. Thus they try to make decisions that will enhance their value and are highly conscious of what others think of their decisions.

3. Steps of the decision-making process:
   a. Identify an existing problem
   b. List possible alternatives for solving the problem
   c. Select the most beneficial of these alternatives
   d. Implement the selected alternative
   e. Gather feedback to find out if the implemented alternative is solving the identified problem

4. Characteristics of conditions of complete certainty, complete uncertainty, and risk:
   a. The **complete certainty condition** exists when decision makers know exactly what the results of an implemented alternative will be. Under this condition, managers have complete knowledge about a decision, so all they have to do is list outcomes for alternatives and then choose the outcome with the highest payoff for the organization.
   b. The **complete uncertainty condition** exists when decision makers have absolutely no idea what the results of an implemented alternative will be. The complete uncertainty condition would exist, for example, if there were no historical data on which to base a decision. Not knowing what happened in the past makes it difficult to predict what will happen in the future.
   c. The primary characteristic of the **risk condition** is that decision makers have only enough information about the outcome of each alternative to estimate how probable an outcome will be. The risk condition is a broad one in which degrees of risk can be associated with decisions. The lower the quality of information about the outcome of an alternative, the closer the situation is to complete uncertainty and the higher is the risk in choosing that alternative.

5. Three primary processes for making group decisions:
   a. **Brainstorming** is a group decision-making process in which negative feedback on any suggested alternative by any group member is forbidden until all members have presented alternatives that they perceive as valuable.
   b. The **nominal group technique** is a group decision-making process in which every group member is assured of equal participation in making the group decision. After each member writes down individual ideas and presents them orally to the group, the entire group discusses all the ideas and then votes for the best idea in a secret ballot.
   c. The **Delphi technique** is a group decision-making process that involves circulating questionnaires on a specific problem among group members, sharing the questionnaire results with them, and them continuing to recirculate and refine individual responses until a consensus regarding the problem is reached.

True-False

1. F	3. T	5. T	7. F	9. T
2. F	4. F	6. T	8. T	10. F

Multiple Choice

1. b	6. b	11. d	16. c	21. b
2. c	7. a	12. a	17. a	22. b
3. c	8. a	13. b	18. b	23. a
4. a	9. b	14. b	19. d	24. d
5. b	10. c	15. c	20. a	25. a

Fill-In

1. computer language
2. higher
3. Decision makers
4. Decision making
5. complete certainty
6. complete uncertainty
7. degrees
8. Probability
9. Brainstorming
10. nominal group technique

Modern Management (9th ed.)
Part 3 - Planning
Chapter Eight – Strategic Planning

Overview

In a turbulent and changing world, organizations need to utilize more than short-term planning to reach their objectives. Strategic planning or the long-term planning that focuses on the organization as a whole is essential. This chapter presents the key concepts and approaches used in strategic planning. The elements of strategic management are noted, as well as the roles that the general, operating, and internal environments play in strategic planning. A variety of approaches such as SWOT and other analytical tools are included.

Chapter Outline

Introductory Case: Gillette's New Strategy: Women

I. STRATEGIC PLANNING

    A. Fundamentals of Strategic Planning

        Strategic planning is long-range planning that focuses on the organization as a whole.

        1. **The Commitment Principle** – a management guideline that advises managers to commit funds for planning only if they can anticipate in the foreseeable future, a return on planning expenses as a result of the long-range planning analysis

        2. **Strategy** – a broad and general plan developed to reach long term organizational objectives; it is the end result of strategic planning

    B. Strategy Management

        Strategy management is the process of ensuring that an organization possesses and benefits from the use of an appropriate organizational strategy.

    C. The strategy management process is generally thought to consist of five sequential and continuing steps:

        1. **Environmental analysis** – the study of the organizational environment to pinpoint environmental factors that can significantly influence organizational operations
            a. General environment
            b. Operating environment
            c. Internal environment

        2. Establishing organizational direction
            a. **Organizational mission** – the purpose for which, or the reason why, and organization exists
            b. **Mission statement** – a written document developed by management, normally based on input by managers as well as nonmanagers, that describes and explains the organization's mission
            c. An organizational mission is very important to an organization because it helps management increase the probability that the organization will be successful.

3. Strategy formulation: Tools

   Strategy formulation is the process of determining appropriate courses of action for achieving organizational objectives and thereby accomplishing organizational purpose. Special tools that managers can use to assist them in formulating strategies include the following:

   a. **Critical question analysis** – a strategy development tool that consists of answering basic questions about the present purposes and objectives of the organization, its present direction and environment, and actions that can be taken to achieve organizational objectives in the future
   b. **SWOT analysis** – a strategy development tool that matches internal organizational strengths and weaknesses with external opportunities and threats.
   c. **Business portfolio analysis** – the development of business-related strategy based primarily on the market share of businesses and the growth of markets in which businesses exist.
      1. The Boston Consulting Group Growth-Share Matrix
      2. The GE Multifactor Portfolio Matrix

   d. Porter's Model for Industry Analysis

3a. Strategy formulation: Types

   The following are the three generic strategies developed by Michael Porter to illustrate the kinds of strategies managers might develop to make their organizations more competitive:

   a. **Differentiation** – a strategy that focuses on making an organization more competitive by developing a product or products that customers perceive as being different from products offered by competitors
   b. **Cost leadership** – a strategy that focuses on making an organization more competitive by producing products more cheaply than competitors can
   c. **Focus** – a strategy that emphasizes making an organization more competitive by targeting a particular customer

3b. Sample organizational strategies

   a. **Growth** – a strategy adopted by management to increase the amount of business that a strategic business unit is currently generating
   b. **Stability** – a strategy adopted by management to maintain or slightly improve the amount of business a strategic business unit is generating
   c. **Retrenchment** – a strategy adopted by management to strengthen or protect the amount of business a strategic business unit is currently generating
   d. **Divestiture** – a strategy adopted to eliminate a strategic business unit that is not generating a satisfactory amount of business and has little hope of doing so in the future

4. Strategy implementation

   The successful implementation of strategy requires four basic skills:
   a. **Interacting skill** – the ability to manage people during implementation
   b. **Allocating skill** – the ability to provide the organizational resources necessary to implement a strategy
   c. **Monitoring skill** – the ability to use information to determine whether a problem has arisen that is blocking implementation
   d. **Organizing skill** – the ability to create throughout the organization a network of people who can help solve implementation problems as they occur

5. Strategic control

   a. Strategic control consists of monitoring and evaluating the strategy management process as a whole to ensure that it is operating properly
   b. Tactical planning – short-range planning that emphasizes the current operations of various parts of the organization

II. PLANNING AND LEVELS OF MANAGEMENT

   A. An organization's top management is primarily responsible for seeing that the planning function is carried count.
   B. Although all management levels are involved in the typical planning process, upper-level mangers usually spend more time planning than lower-level managers do.

Test Your Knowledge

Essay

1. List and discuss the five major components of an organization's operating environment. (p. 173)

2. Discuss the four basic questions that are essential in formulating an appropriate organizational strategy based on the process of critical question analysis. (p. 176)

3. List and discuss four matrix quadrants into which a strategic business unit (SBU) can be categorized according to the Boston Consulting Matrix. (p. 177)

4. List and describe the three generic strategies, according to Michael Porter, which will make companies more competitive within an industry. (p. 179)

5. Discuss the four basic skills that successful implementation of strategy requires. (p. 182)

True-False

T F 1. Gender issues were at the heart of Gillette's new strategy. (p. 167)

T F 2. A strategic plan is for less than one year. (p. 168)

T F 3. Strategy is defined as a narrow and specific plan to reach long-term goals. (p. 168)

Chapter Eight – Strategic Planning

T F   4. Strategic management is a process. (p. 169)

T F   5. The first step in strategic management is to establish organizational direction. (p. 169)

T F   6. The general environment consists of labor, customers, and competitors. (p. 171)

T F   7. The organizational mission is the purpose for which the organization exists. (p. 174)

T F   8. The S in the SWOT analysis stands for strategy. (p. 177)

T F   9. An SBU is a strategic business unit. (p. 177)

T F   10. Among the strategies that organizations can use is retrenchment. (p. 179)

Multiple Choice

1. Strategic planning is what among the following descriptors? (p. 168)
    a. Long-range
    b. Short-range
    c. Easy
    d. None are correct

2. _____ is the end result of strategic planning. (p. 168)
    a. Policies
    b. Procedures
    c. Strategy
    d. Rules

3. Strategy is_____and_____. (p. 168)
    a. broad and general
    b. specific and directional
    c. specific and short-term
    d. broad and narrow

4. Which of the following is the first step in the strategy management process? (p. 169)
    a. environmental analysis
    b. establishment of an organizational direction
    c. strategy formulation
    d. strategy implementation

5. Strategic management generally is thought to consist of 5 separate sequential and continuing steps. Which of the following apply? (p. 169)
    a. Environmental analysis
    b. Strategy formulation
    c. Strategy implementation
    d. All apply

6. The organization's operating environment consists of all but which of the following? (p. 173)
    a. Economics
    b. Labor
    c. Competition
    d. Customer

Chapter Eight – Strategic Planning

7. Technology is a part of which environment? (p. 171)
    a. General
    b. Specific
    c. Organizational
    d. None are correct

8. The _____ environment is the level of an organization's external environment that contains components normally having broad long-term implications for managing the organization. (p. 170)
    a. general
    b. operating
    c. internal
    d. cultural

9. Which of the following is not considered a component of the general environment? (p. 171)
    a. economic
    b. social
    c. political
    d. suppliers

10. _____ is the science that focuses on understanding how people of a particular community or nation produce, distribute, and use various goods and services. (p. 171)
    a. Demographics
    b. Psychographics
    c. Economics
    d. Culturalism

11. The statistical characteristics of a population are referred to as _____. (p. 172)
    a. demographics
    b. psychographics
    c. economics
    d. culturalism

12. The _____ is the part of the environment that usually has immediate and specific implications for managing the organization. (p. 173)
    a. external
    b. internal
    c. upper management
    d. worker

13. _____ are individuals or agencies that provide organizations with the resources they need to produce goods and services. (p. 173)
    a. Consumers
    b. Distributors
    c. Suppliers
    d. Employees

Chapter Eight – Strategic Planning

14. The organizational _____ is the purpose for which the organization exists. (p. 174)
    a. mission
    b. management
    c. environment
    d. None are correct

15. A written document development by management, normally based on input by managers as well as nonmanagers, that describes and explains the organization's mission is called a(n) _____. (p. 174)
    a. organizational hierarchy
    b. employee handbook
    c. mission statement
    d. standing plan

16. Which among the following are included as strategy formulation tools? (p. 176)
    a. Critical question analysis
    b. SWOT
    c. Business portfolio analysis
    d. All are correct

17. The O in SWOT stands for what? (p. 177)
    a. Organization
    b. Organizational
    c. Order
    d. Opportunity

18. Which of the following is part of the SBU analysis? (p. 177)
    a. Cash cows
    b. Stars
    c. Question marks
    d. All are correct

19. _____ is a strategy that focuses on making an organization more competitive by developing a product that customers perceive as being different from products offered by competitors. (p. 179)
    a. Differentiation
    b. Cost leadership
    c. Focus
    d. Stability

20. Which of the following strategies focuses on making an organization more competitive by producing products more cheaply than competitors can? (p. 180)
    a. Differentiation
    b. Cost leadership
    c. Focus
    d. Stability

Chapter Eight – Strategic Planning

21. _____ is a strategy that emphasizes making an organization more competitive by targeting a particular customer. (p. 180)
    a. Differentiation
    b. Cost leadership
    c. Focus
    d. Stability

22. Which of the following strategies is adopted by management to maintain or slightly improve the amount of business a strategic business unit is generating? (p. 181)
    a. Differentiation
    b. Cost leadership
    c. Focus
    d. Stability

23. _____ is a strategy adopted by management to strengthen or protect the amount of business a strategic business unit is currently generating. (p. 181)
    a. Differentiation
    b. Cost leadership
    c. Retrenchment
    d. Stability

24. Which of the following is a strategy adopted to a eliminate a strategic business unit that is not generating a satisfactory amount of business and has little hope of doing so in the future? (p. 181)
    a. Differentiation
    b. Cost leadership
    c. Divesture
    d. Stability

25. _____ is short-range planning that emphasizes the current operations of various parts of the organization. (p. 183)
    a. Corporate planning
    b. Tactical planning
    c. Operations management
    d. Policy development

Fill-In

1. _____ is long-range planning that focuses on the organization as a whole. (p. 168)

2. _____ is actually the end result of strategic planning. (p. 169)

3. The study of the organizational environment to pinpoint environmental factors that can significantly influence organizational operations is called _____. (p. 170)

4. The social component is part of the _____ that describes the characteristics of the society in which the organization exists. (p. 171)

5. _____ are the relative degrees of worth that society places on the ways in which it exists and functions. (p. 172)

6. The _____ component is the operating environment segment that is composed of those with whom an organization must battle in order to obtain resources. (p. 173)

7. The most common initial act in establishing organizational direction is determining a(n) _____. (p. 174)

8. _____ is a strategic development tool that matches internal organizational strengths and weaknesses with external opportunities and threats. (p. 177)

9. An organizational strategy formulation technique that is based on the philosophy that organizations should develop strategy much as they handle investment portfolios is called _____. (p. 177)

10. A(n) _____ is a significant organization segment that is analyzed to develop organizational strategy aimed at generating future business or revenue. (p. 177)

Answers

Essay

1. The five major components of an organization's operating environment
    a. The **customer component** is the operating environment segment that is composed of factors relating to those who buy goods and services provided by the organization.
    b. The **competition component** is the operating environment segment that is composed of those with whom an organization must battle in order to obtain resources.
    c. The **labor component** is the operating environment segment that is composed of factors influencing the supply of workers available to perform needed organizational tasks.
    d. The **supplier component** is the operating environment segment that comprises all variables related to the individuals or agencies that provide organization with the resources they need to produce goods or services.
    e. The **international component** is the operating environment segment that is composed of all the factors relating to the international implications of organizational operations.

2. Four basic questions that are essential in formulating an appropriate organizational strategy
    a. What are the purposes and objective of the organization? The answer to this question will tell management where the organization should be going. By answering this question during the strategy formulation process, managers are likely to remember this important point and thereby minimize inconsistencies among the organization's purposes, objectives, and strategies.
    b. Where is the organization presently going? The answer to this question can tell managers if the organization is achieving its goals, and if it is, whether the level of progress is satisfactory. Whereas the first question focused on where the organization should be going, this one focuses on where the organization is actually going.
    c. In what king of environment does the organization now exist? Both internal and external environments are covered in this question. Any strategy formulated, if it to be appropriate, must deal with these factors.
    d. What can be done to better achieve organizational objectives in the future? It is the answer to this question that results in the strategy of the organization. Managers cannot develop an appropriate organizational strategy unless they have a clear understanding of where the organization wants to go, where it is going, and in what environment it exists.

3. <u>Four matrix quadrants into which an SBU can be categorized</u>
   a. **Stars**—SBUs that are "stars" have a high share of a high-growth market and typically need large amounts of cash to support their rapid and significant growth. Stars also generate large amounts of cash for the organization and are usually segments in which management can make additional investments and earn attractive returns.
   b. **Cash Cows**—SBUs that are "cash cows" have a large share of a market that is growing only slightly. These SBUs provide the organization with large amounts of cash, but since their market is not growing significantly, the case is generally used to meet the financial demands of the organization in other areas, such as the expansion of a star SBU.
   c. **Question Marks**—SBUs that are "question marks" have a small share of a high-growth market. They are dubbed "question marks" because it is uncertain whether management should invest more cash in them to gain a larger share of the market or deemphasize or eliminate them. Management will chose the first option when it believes it can turn the question mark into a star, and the second when it thinks further investment would be fruitless.
   d. **Dogs**—SBUs that are dogs have a relatively small share of a low-growth market. They may barely support themselves; in some cases, they actually drain off cash resources generated by other SBUs. Examples of dogs are SBUs that produce typewriters or cash registers.

4. <u>Three generic competitive strategies that will make companies more competitive</u>
   a. **Differentiation**—a strategy that focuses on making an organization more competitive by developing a product or products that customers perceive as being different from products offered by competitors.
   b. **Cost leadership**—a strategy that focuses on making an organization more competitive by producing product more cheaply than competitors can. According to the logic behind this strategy, by producing products more cheaply than its competitors do, an organization will be able to offer products to customers at lower prices than competitors can.
   c. **Focus**—a strategy that emphasizes making an organization more competitive by targeting a particular customer. Magazine companies commonly use a focus strategy in offering their products to specific customers.

5. <u>Four basic skills that successful implementation of strategy requires</u>
   a. **Interacting skill** is the ability to manage people during implementation. Managers who are able to understand the fears and frustrations others feel during the implementation of a new strategy tend to be the best implementers.
   b. **Allocating skill** is the ability to provide organizational resources necessary to implement a strategy. Successful implementers are talented at scheduling jobs, budgeting time and money, and allocating other resources that are critical for implementation.
   c. **Monitoring skill** is the ability to use information to determine whether a problem has arisen that is blocking implementation. Good strategy implementers set up feedback systems that continually tell them about the status of strategy implementation.
   d. **Organizing skill** is the ability to create throughout the organization a network of people who can help solve implementation problems as they occur. Good implementers customize this network to include individuals who can handle the special types of problems anticipated in the implementation of a particular package.

Chapter Eight – Strategic Planning

True-False

1. T
2. F
3. F
4. T
5. F
6. F
7. T
8. F
9. T
10. T

Multiple Choice

1. a
2. c
3. a
4. a
5. c
6. a
7. a
8. a
9. d
10. c
11. a
12. b
13. c
14. a
15. c
16. d
17. d
18. d
19. a
20. b
21. c
22. d
23. c
24. c
25. b

Fill-In

1. Strategic planning
2. Strategy
3. environmental analysis
4. general environment
5. Social values
6. competition
7. organizational mission
8. SWOT analysis
9. business portfolio analysis
10. strategic business unit

Modern Management (9th ed.)
Part 3 - Planning
Chapter Nine – Plans and Planning Tools

Overview

This chapter introduces the types of plans that are available, the use of the various plans, insights into why plans sometimes fail, the use of forecasting, and the advantages and disadvantages of sales forecasting. Also included is a discussion of scheduling and the uses of Gantt charts and PERT.

Chapter Outline

Introductory Case: Ford Plans to Improve the Explorer

I. PLANS: A DEFINITION

    A **plan** is a specific action proposed to help the organization achieve its objectives.

    A. Dimensions of Plans
        1. **Repetitiveness** – the repetitiveness dimension of a plan is the extent to which the plan is to be used over and over again
        2. **Time** – the time dimension of a plan is the length of time that plan covers
        3. **Scope** – the scope dimension of a plan is the portion of the total management system at which the plan is aimed
        4. **Level** – the level dimension of a plan is the level of the organization at which the plan is aimed

    B. Types of Plans

        1. Standing plans
            a. **Policy** – a standing plan that furnishes broad guidelines for channeling management toward taking action consistent with reaching organizational objectives
            b. **Procedure** – a standing plan that outlines a series of related actions that must be taken to accomplish a particular task
            c. **Rule** – a standing plan that designates a specific required action

        2. Single-use plans
            a. **Program** – a single-use plan designed to carry out a special project in an organization that, if accomplished, will contribute to the organization's long-term success
            b. **Budget** – a control tool that outlines how funds in a given period will be spent, as well as how they will be obtained

    C. Why Plans Fail

        There are a number of reasons that plans fail. The following are a list of the ten most common reasons:
        1. Corporate planning is not fully integrated into the total management system.
        2. There is a lack of understanding of the different steps of the planning process.
        3. Lack of engagement by all involved managers.
        4. Responsibility for planning is wrongly vested solely in the planning department.
        5. Management expects that plans developed will be realized with little effort.
        6. In starting formal planning, too much is attempted at once.

7. Management fails to operate by the plan.
8. Financial projections are confused with planning.
9. Inadequate inputs are used in planning.
10. Management fails to grasp the overall planning process.

D. Planning Areas: Input planning

Input planning is the development of proposed action that will furnish sufficient and appropriate organizational resources for reaching established organizational objectives.

1. **Plant facilities planning** – input planning that involves developing the type of work facility an organization will need to reach its objectives
2. **Site selection** – involves determining where a plan facility should be located. It may use a weighting process to compare site differences
3. **Human resource planning** – input planning that involves obtaining the human resources necessary for the organization to achieve its objectives

II. PLANNING TOOLS

Planning tools are techniques managers can use to help develop plans.

A. **Forecasting** – a planning tool used to predict future environmental happenings that will influence the operation of the organization

B. Methods for Sales Forecasting
1. **Jury of Executive Opinion Method** – a method of predicting future sales levels primarily by asking appropriate managers to give their opinions on what will happen to sales in the future
2. **Salesforce Estimation Method** – predicts future sales levels primarily by asking appropriate salespeople for their opinions of what will happen to sales in the future
3. **Time Series Analysis Method** – a method of predicting future sales levels by analyzing the historical relationship in an organization between sales and time

C. Scheduling

Scheduling is the process of formulating a detailed listing of activities that must be accomplished to attain an objective, allocating the resources necessary to attain the objective, and setting up and following timetables for completing the objective.

1. **Gantt Charts** – a scheduling tool composed of a bar chart with time on the horizontal axis and the resource to be scheduled on the vertical axis. It is used for scheduling resources.
2. **Program Evaluation and Review Technique (PERT)** – a scheduling tool that is essentially a network of project activities showing estimates of time necessary to complete each activity and the sequence of activities that must be followed to complete the project.
   a. **Activities** – specified sets of behavior within a project
   b. **Events** – the completions of major project tasks
   c. **Critical Path** – the sequence of events and activities within a PERT network that requires the longest period of time to complete

Chapter Nine – Plans and Planning Tools

Test Your Knowledge

Essay

1. List and discuss the four major dimensions of plans. (p. 192)

2. In a short essay, define a policy, a procedure, and a rule. (p. 194)

3. List at least five specific reasons why plans fail. (p. 196)

4. Discuss the characteristics of the following methods of sales forecasting: the jury of executive opinion method, the salesforce estimation method, and the time series analysis method. (p. 200)

5. Define PERT and list the four primary steps that managers should follow when designing a PERT network. (p. 205)

True-False

T F 1. All planning is foolproof. (p. 191)

T F 2. A plan is very general in its structure. (p. 192)

T F 3. Toyota is using a philanthropy plan to take aim at General Motors. (p. 192)

T F 4. One dimension of a plan is complexity. (p. 192)

T F 5. A type of standing plan is a budget. (p. 194)

T F 6. Luckily, Salomon Smith Barney had no problems integrating the Internet into the firm. (p. 195)

T F 7. A budget is a control tool. (p. 196)

T F 8. An aspect of plant facilities planning is site selection. (p. 196)

T F 9. Forecasting predicts the future accurately without fail. (p. 200)

T F 10. A product has three life cycles. (p. 202)

Multiple Choice

1. What automobile company is Toyota aiming at? (p. 192)
    a. Ford
    b. Volvo
    c. Honda
    d. General Motors

2. Which of the following are considered dimensions of plans? (p. 192)
    a. Repetitiveness
    b. Time
    c. Scope
    d. All are correct

3. The _____ dimension of a plan is the extent to which the plan is to be used over and over again. (p. 192)
   a. repetitiveness
   b. time
   c. scope
   d. intensity

4. Which of the following dimensions of a plan is the portion of the total management system at which the plan is aimed? (p. 192)
   a. repetitiveness
   b. time
   c. scope
   d. level

5. The _____ dimension of the plan is the portion of the total management system at which the plan is aimed. (p. 192)
   a. time
   b. scope
   c. level
   d. None are correct

6. Which of the following are plans that are used over and over because they focus on organizational situations that occur repeatedly? (p. 194)
   a. standing plans
   b. single-use plans
   c. cross-over plans
   d. concurrent plans

7. _____ are plans that are used only mostly once because they focus on unique or rare situations within the organization. (p. 194)
   a. Standing plans
   b. Single-use plans
   c. Cross-over plans
   d. Concurrent plans

8. A _____ is a standing plan that furnishes broad guidelines. (p. 194)
   a. rule
   b. procedure
   c. policy
   d. guide

9. Which of the following is a standing plan that outlines a series of related actions that must be taken to accomplish a particular task? (p. 195)
   a. a rule
   b. a procedure
   c. a policy
   d. a program

Chapter Nine – Plans and Planning Tools

10. A(n) _____ is a single-use plan designed to carry out a special project (p. 195)
    in an organization that will contribute to the organization's long-term success.
    a. a rule
    b. a procedure
    c. a policy
    d. a program

11. A budget is a _____ tool. (p. 196)
    a. control
    b. policy
    c. rule
    d. None are correct

12. _____ is the development of proposed action that will furnish sufficient and (p. 196)
    appropriate organizational resources for reaching established organizational objectives.
    a. Output planning
    b. Input planning
    c. Site selection
    d. Critical control analysis

13. Which of the following types of planning is input planning that involves developing (p. 196)
    the type of work facility an organization will need to reach its objectives?
    a. plant facilities planning
    b. output planning
    c. input planning
    d. critical control analysis

14. _____ involves determining where a plan facility should be located. (p. 196)
    a. Output planning
    b. Input planning
    c. Site selection
    d. PERT analysis

15. _____ is input planning that involves obtaining the human resources (p. 198)
    necessary for the organization to achieve its objectives.
    a. Strategy planning
    b. Business development
    c. Human resource planning
    d. Market development

16. _____ attempts to predict the future. (p. 200)
    a. Forecasting
    b. PERT
    c. Gantt Charts
    d. None are correct

Chapter Nine – Plans and Planning Tools

17. Which of the following are types of sales forecasting tools? (p. 200)
    a. Jury of executive opinion
    b. Salesforce estimation
    c. Time series analysis
    d. All are correct

18. The _____ method is a method of predicting future sales level primarily by asking appropriate managers to give their opinions on what will happen to sales in the future. (p. 200)
    a. jury of executive opinion
    b. salesforce estimation
    c. time series analysis
    d. correlation forecasting

19. Which of the following forecasting methods predicts future sales levels primarily by asking appropriate salespeople for their opinions of what will happen to sales in the future? (p. 200)
    a. jury of executive opinion method
    b. salesforce estimation method
    c. time series analysis method
    d. correlation forecasting method

20. The _____ method is a method of predicting future sales levels by analyzing the historical relationship in an organization between sales and time. (p. 200)
    a. jury of executive opinion
    b. salesforce estimation
    c. time series analysis
    d. correlation forecasting

21. A product has how many life cycles? (p. 202)
    a. 1
    b. 3
    c. 5
    d. 7

22. The _____ is a scheduling tool composed of a bar chart with time on the horizontal axis and the resource to be scheduled on the vertical axis. (p. 203)
    a. Gantt chart
    b. time series chart
    c. correlation chart
    d. regression chart

23. Which of the following is a network of project activities showing both the estimates of time necessary to complete each activity and the sequence of activities that must be followed to complete the project? (p. 204)
    a. Gantt Chart
    b. PERT
    c. correlation chart
    d. regression chart

Chapter Nine – Plans and Planning Tools

24. In a PERT network, _____ are specified sets of behavior within a project. (p. 204)
    a. activities
    b. events
    c. rules
    d. procedures

25. Which of the following are the completions of major project tasks in a PERT network? (p. 204)
    a. activities
    b. events
    c. critical path
    d. procedures

Fill-In

1. A(n) _____ is a specific action proposed to help the organization achieve its objectives. (p. 192)

2. The _____ of a plan is the level of the organization at which the plan is aimed. (p. 193)

3. _____ can be subdivided into policies, procedures and rules. (p. 194)

4. A standing plan that designates specific required action is called a(n) _____. (p. 195)

5. An example of a(n) _____ that many companies are now establishing is "No Smoking." (p. 195)

6. One factor that significantly influences site selection is _____. (p. 196)

7. A(n) _____ is a prediction of how high or low sales of the organization's products and/or services will be over the period of time under consideration. (p. 200)

8. The five stages through which most products and services pass is called a(n) _____. (p. 202)

9. _____ is the process of formulating a detailed listing of activities that must be accomplished to attain an objective. (p. 203)

10. The _____ helps managers predict which features of a schedule are becoming unrealistic and provides insights into how those features might be eliminated or modified. (p. 205)

Chapter Nine – Plans and Planning Tools

Answers

Essay

1. Dimensions of plans include the following:
   a. The **repetitiveness dimension** of a plan is the extent to which the plan is used over and over again. Some plans are specially designed for one situation that is relatively short term in nature. Plans of this sort are essentially nonrepetitive. Other plans are designed to be used time after time for long-term recurring situations. These plans are basically repetitive in nature.
   b. The **time dimension** of a plan is the length of time the plan covers. Strategic planning is defined as long term in nature, while tactical planning is defined as short term. Strategic plans cover relatively long periods of time and tactical plans cover relatively short periods of time.
   c. The **scope dimension** of a plan is the portion of the total management system at which the plan is aimed. Some plans are designed to cover the entire open management system: the organizational environment, inputs, process, and outputs. Such a plan is often referred to as a master plan.
   d. The **level dimension** of a plan is the level of the organization at which the plan is aimed. Top-level plans are those designed for the organization's top management, whereas middle-and lower-level plans are designed for middle and lower management, respectively.

2. A **policy** is a standing plan that furnishes broad guidelines for channeling management toward taking action consistent with reaching organizational objectives. A **procedure** is a standing plan that outlines a series of related actions that must be taken to accomplish a particular task. In general, procedures outline more specific actions than policies do. A **rule** is a standing plan that designates specific required action. In essence, a rule indicates what an organization member should or should not do and allows no room for interpretation.

3. <u>Reasons why plans fail</u>
   a. Corporate planning is not integrated into the total management system
   b. There is a lack of understanding of the different steps of the planning process
   c. Management at different levels in the organization has not properly engaged in or contributed to planning activities
   d. Responsibility for planning is wrongly vested solely in the planning department
   e. Management expects that plans developed will be realized with little effort
   f. In starting formal planning, too much is attempted at once
   g. Management fails to operate by the plan
   h. Financial projections are confused with planning
   i. Inadequate inputs are used in planning
   j. Management fails to grasp the overall planning process

Chapter Nine – Plans and Planning Tools

4. Methods of forecasting
    a. The **jury of executive opinion method** is a method of predicting future sales levels primarily by asking appropriate managers to give their opinions on what will happen to sales in the future. Since these discussion sessions usually revolve around hunches or experienced guesses, the resulting forecast is a blend of informed opinions.
    b. The **salesforce estimation method** predicts future sales levels primarily by asking appropriate salespeople for their opinions of what will happen to sales in the future. Salespeople continually interact with customers, and from this interaction they usually develop a knack for predicting future sales.
    c. The **time series analysis method** is a method of predicting future sales levels by analyzing the historical relationship in an organization between sales and time. Information showing the relationship between sales and time typically is presented on a graph.

5. The **program evaluation and review technique (PERT)** is a scheduling tool that is essentially a network of project activities showing estimates of time necessary to complete each activity and the sequence of activities that must be followed to complete the project. When designing a PERT network, managers should follow four primary steps:
    a. Step 1—list all the activities/events that must be accomplished for the project and the sequence in which these activities/events should be performed
    b. Step 2—determine how much time will be needed to complete each activity/event
    c. Step 3—design a PERT network that reflects all of the information contained in steps 1 and 2
    d. Step 4—identify the critical path

True-False

1. F
2. F
3. T
4. F
5. F
6. F
7. T
8. T
9. F
10. F

Multiple Choice

1. d
2. d
3. a
4. c
5. b
6. a
7. b
8. c
9. b
10. d
11. a
12. b
13. a
14. c
15. c
16. a
17. d
18. a
19. b
20. c
21. c
22. a
23. b
24. a
25. b

Fill-In

1. plan
2. level dimension
3. Standing plans
4. rule
5. rule
6. foreign location
7. sales forecast
8. product life cycle
9. Scheduling
10. critical path

Modern Management (9th ed.)
Part 4 - Organizing
Chapter Ten – Fundamentals of Organizing

Overview

This chapter will introduce you to the concepts of organizing work through the structuring of the organization. The importance of organizing, the process, the subsystem, and the classical theories that the concepts organizing are structured on will be covered. Issues of division of labor, span of management, and scalar relationships will also be presented.

Chapter Outline

Introductory Case: Lucent Technologies Organizes for to Be More Competitive

I. A DEFINITION OF ORGANIZING

   A. **Organizing** is the process of establishing orderly uses for all the organization's resources. An organization is the result of the organizing process.

      1. Fayol developed 16 organizational guidelines for organizing resources.

   B. The Importance of Organizing

      1. The organizing function is the primary mechanism used by managers to activate plans.

   C. The Organizing Process

      1. There are 5 steps in the organizing process.
         a. reflect on plans and objectives
         b. establish major tasks
         c. divide major tasks into subtasks
         d. allocate resources and directives for subtasks
         e. evaluate the results of implemented organized strategy

   D. The Organizing Subsystem

      1. The primary purpose of the subsystem is to enhance goal attainment.

II. CLASSICAL ORGANIZING THEORY

   A. **Classical organizing theory** comprises the cumulative insights of early management writers on how organizational resources can best be used to enhance goal achievement.

   B. Weber's Bureaucratic Model

   Bureaucracy is a term Max Weber used to describe a management system characterized by detailed procedures and rules, a clearly outlined organizational hierarchy, and impersonal relationships among organization members.

Chapter Ten – Fundamentals of Organizing

C. Structure
1. Structure
2. Organizational chart
3. Authority and Responsibility
4. Structure and gender
5. Formal and informal structure
6. Departmentalization and Formal Structure: A Contingency Viewpoint

    a. Functional departmentalization
    b. Product departmentalization
    c. Geographic departmentalization
    d. Customer departmentalization
    e. Manufacturing process departmentalization
    f. Forces influencing formal structure

D. Division of Labor

1. Division of labor is the assignment of various portions of a particular task among a number of organizational members
2. Division of labor calls for specialization
3. Division of labor and coordination
4. Follett's Guidelines on Coordination

E. Span of Management

1. The span of management refers to the number of individuals a manager supervises.

2. Designing span of management: a contingency view
    a. Similarity of functions
    b. Geographic continuity
    c. Complexity of functions
    d. Coordination
    e. Planning

3. Graicunas and span of management

    Graicunas' formula – a formula that makes the span-of-management point that as the number of a manager's subordinates increases arithmetically, the number of possible relationships between the manager and the subordinates increases geometrically

4. Height of organization chart—flat or tall

    a. A **flat organization chart** is an organization chart characterized by few levels and a relatively broad span of management.
    b. A **tall organization chart** is an organization chart characterized by many levels and relatively narrow span of management.

Chapter Ten – Fundamentals of Organizing

    F. Scalar Relationships

        1. **Scalar relationships** refer to the chain-of-command positioning of individuals on an organization chart and unity of command.
        2. **Unity of command** is the management principle that recommends that an individual have only one boss.
        3. Fayol's guidelines on chain of command and the gangplank
            a. **Gangplank** – a communication channel extending from one organizational division to another but not shown in the lines of communication outlined on an organization chart

Test Your Knowledge

Essays

1. List the five main steps of the organizing process. (p. 215)

2. Identify the two basic types of structure within management systems and compare the characteristics of each system. (p. 218)

3. Define span of management and discuss the central concern regarding this concept. (p. 224)

4. List and discuss the five situational factors that influence the appropriateness of the size of an individual's span of management. (p. 225)

5. Define scalar relationships and discuss the concept of unity of command. (p. 226)

True-False

T F 1. Making use of sanctions against faults and errors is one of Fayol's 16 principles. (p. 214)

T F 2. A key to organizing is the orderly use of resources. (p. 214)

T F 3. Fayol's 16 points argue for an unconventional approach to organization. (p. 214)

T F 4. The first step in the organizing process is to establish the major tasks. (p. 215)

T F 5. One aspect of the organizing subsystem is input. (p. 216)

T F 6. Input, process, and output are all parts of the organizing subsystem. (p. 216)

T F 7. The organizational chart is a verbal representation of the structure. (p. 218)

T F 8. Some authors argue that women create different structures than do men. (p. 218)

T F 9. Geographical departmentalization is based primarily on territory. (p. 219)

T F 10. Division of labor calls for specialization. (p. 223)

Chapter Ten – Fundamentals of Organizing

Multiple Choice

1. Lucent was originally structured with what company? (p. 213)
   a. IBM
   b. Apple
   c. Sun Microsystems
   d. AT&T

2. What is referred to as the result of the organizing process? (p. 214)
   a. Structure
   b. Procedures
   c. Organization
   d. None are correct

3. Which of the following are among Fayol's 16 principles? (p. 214)
   a. Avoid regulations, red tape and paperwork
   b. Make use of sanctions against faults and errors
   c. Define duties
   d. All are correct

4. Which of the following is *not* a part of the organizing subsystem? (p. 216)
   a. Input
   b. Process
   c. Output
   d. Transition

5. Which classical theorist is most aligned with the organizational structure of the bureaucracy? (p. 217)
   a. Fayol
   b. Follett
   c. Weber
   d. Barnard

6. _____ is the term Max Weber used to describe a management system characterized by detailed procedures and rules and impersonal relationships among organization members. (p. 217)
   a. Decentralization
   b. Bureaucracy
   c. Authority
   d. Empowerment

7. Which of the following refers to the designed relationships among resources of the management system? (p. 218)
   a. planning
   b. communication
   c. structure
   d. authority

Chapter Ten – Fundamentals of Organizing

8. Some contend that women structure organizations differently. Which of the following terms best describes that structure? (p. 218)
   a. Networks or webs
   b. Hierarchies based on gender
   c. Circles
   d. None are correct

9. _____ is defined as the relationships among organizational resources as outlined by management. (p. 218)
   a. Formal structure
   b. Informal structure
   c. Innovation
   d. Responsibility

10. Functional departmentalization deals with the type of _____. (p. 218)
    a. work functions
    b. products
    c. people
    d. geography

11. A(n) _____ is a unique group of resources established by management to perform some organizational task. (p. 219)
    a. network
    b. organization structure
    c. procedure
    d. department

12. _____ is the process of establishing departments within the management system. (p. 219)
    a. Delegation
    b. Empowerment
    c. Departmentalization
    d. Decentralization

13. One of the factors stressed by Mary Parker Follett was _____. (p. 223)
    a. very strict communication patterns
    b. no team approaches
    c. personal communication
    d. management hierarchy

14. _____ is the assignment of various portions of a particular task among a number of organization members. (p. 223)
    a. Unity of command
    b. Division of labor
    c. Empowerment
    d. Bureaucracy

Chapter Ten – Fundamentals of Organizing

15. The span of management deals with what? (p. 224)
    a. The number of products the manager manages.
    b. The types of control the manager uses.
    c. The number of rules the organization establishes.
    d. The number of people the manager supervises.

16. The degree to which workers' activities are difficult and involved is referred to as which of the following situational factors that influence the size of an individual's span of management? (p. 225)
    a. similarity of functions
    b. geographic continuity
    c. complexity of functions
    d. coordination

17. Which of the following situational factors that influence the size of an individual's span of management refers to the amount of time managers must spend synchronizing the activities of their subordinates with the activities of other workers? (p. 225)
    a. coordination
    b. similarity of functions
    c. geographic continuity
    d. complexity of functions

18. A _____ organizational chart has few levels. (p. 226)
    a. tall
    b. flat
    c. hierarchical
    d. None are correct

19. Which of the following is characterized by many levels and a relatively narrow span of management? (p. 226)
    a. flat organization chart
    b. tall organization chart
    c. scalar organization chart
    d. decentralized organization chart

20. _____ refer to the chain-of-command positioning of individuals on an organization chart. (p. 226)
    a. Unity of command
    b. Scalar relationships
    c. Bureaucracy
    d. Centralization

Fill-In

1. Traditionally, an organization chart is constructed in _____ form, with individuals toward the top having more authority and responsibility than those toward the bottom. (p. 218)

2. _____ is defined as the patterns of relationships that develop because of the informal activities of organization members. (p. 219)

Chapter Ten – Fundamentals of Organizing

3. Perhaps the most widely used basis for establishing departments within the formal structure is the type of _____ being performed within the management system. (p. 219)

4. Structure based primarily on _____ departmentalizes according to the places where the work is being done. (p. 219)

5. _____ include the degree of technology involved in performing the task and the task's complexity. (p. 221)

6. A commonly used illustration of division of labor is the _____ production line. (p. 223)

7. _____ involves encouraging the completion of individual portions of a task an appropriate, synchronized order. (p. 223)

8. _____ provided valuable advice on how managers can establish and maintain coordination within the organization. (p. 223)

9. The more individuals a manager supervises, the _____ the span of management. (p. 224)

10. The degree to which subordinates are physically separated is referred to as _____. (p. 225)

Answers

Essay

1. The five main steps of the organizing process are as follows:
    a. Reflect on plans and objectives
    b. Establish major tasks
    c. Divide major tasks into subtasks
    d. Allocate resources and directives for subtasks
    e. Evaluate the results of implemented organizing strategy

2. The two basic types of structure within management systems are formal and informal. **Formal structure** is defined as the relationship among organizational resources as outlined by management. It is represented primarily by the organization chart. **Informal structure** is defined as the patterns of relationships that develop because of the informal activities of organization members. It evolves naturally and tends to be molded by individual norms and values and social relationships.

3. The **span of management** is the number of individuals a manager supervises. The more individuals a manager supervises, the greater the span of management. Conversely, the fewer individuals a manager supervises, the smaller the span of management. The span of management has a significant effect on how well managers carry out their responsibilities. The *central concern* of span of management is to determine how many individuals a manager can supervise effectively.

4. The appropriateness of the size of an individual's span of management are as follows:
    a. *Similarity of functions* – the degree to which activities performed by supervised individuals are similar or dissimilar
    b. *Geographic continuity* – the degree to which subordinates are physically separated
    c. *Complexity of functions* – the degree to which workers' activities are difficult and involved
    d. *Coordination* – the amount of time managers must spend synchronizing the activities of their subordinates with the activities of other workers
    e. *Planning* – the amount of time managers must spend developing management system objectives and plans and integrating them with the activities of their subordinates

Chapter Ten – Fundamentals of Organizing

5. **Scalar relationships** refer to the chain-of-command positioning of individuals on an organization chart. The scalar relationship, or chain of command, is related to the unity of command. **Unity of command** is the management principle that recommends that an individual have only one boss. If too many bosses give orders, the result will probably be confusion, contradiction, and frustration—a sure recipe for ineffectiveness and inefficiency in an organization.

True-False

1. T
2. T
3. F
4. F
5. T
6. T
7. F
8. T
9. T
10. T

Multiple Choice

1. d
2. c
3. d
4. d
5. c
6. b
7. c
8. a
9. a
10. a
11. d
12. c
13. c
14. b
15. d
16. c
17. a
18. b
19. b
20. b

Fill-In

1. pyramid
2. Informal structure
3. work functions
4. territory
5. Forces in the task
6. automobile
7. Coordination
8. Mary Parker Follett
9. greater
10. geographic continuity

Modern Management (9th ed.)
Part 4 – Organizing
Chapter Eleven – Responsibility, Authority, and Delegation

Overview

The chapter discusses the concepts of responsibility, authority, and delegation as they impact management. Each is defined and explained in relationship to other concepts. The issue of conflict is presented, as well as insights into accountability, delegation, and decentralization.

Chapter Outline

Introductory Case: Organizing P&G's New Internet Push

I. RESPONSIBILITY

   Responsibility is defined as the obligation to perform assigned activities.

   A. The Job Description

   A **job description** is a list of specific activities that must be performed to accomplish some task or job.

   B. Dividing Job Activities

   1. The **functional similarity** method is a method for dividing job activities in the organization.

   2. This method suggests that management should take four basic interrelated steps to divide job activities.

      a. Examine management system objectives
      b. Designate appropriate activities that must be performed to reach those objectives
      c. Design specific jobs by grouping similar activities
      d. Make specific individuals responsible for performing those jobs

   3. Functional similarity and responsibility

      a. **Overlapping responsibility** – refers to a situation in which more than one individual is responsible for the same activity
      b. **Responsibility gap** – exist when certain organizational tasks are not included in the responsibility are of any individual organizational member
      c. When two or more employees are uncertain as to who is responsible for a task, four outcomes are possible:

         1. One of the two may perform the job.
         2. Both employees may perform the job.
         3. Neither employee may perform the job because each assumed the other would complete the task.
         4. The employees may spend valuable time negotiating each aspect and phase of the job to carefully mesh their job responsibilities, thus minimizing both duplication of effort and responsibility gaps.

C. Clarifying Job Activities of Managers

1. **Management Responsibility Guide** – a tool that is used to clarify the responsibilities of various managers in the organization
2. **Responsible managers** – managers can be described as responsible if they perform the activities they are obligated to perform
3. The degree of responsibility that a manager possesses can be determined by appraising the manager on the following four dimensions:

   a. Attitude toward and conduct with subordinates
   b. Behavior with upper management
   c. Behavior with other groups
   d. Personal attitudes and values

II. AUTHORITY

A. Authority is defined as the right to perform or command.

B. **Authority on the job** – practically speaking, authority merely increases the probability that a specific command will be obeyed

C. Acceptance of authority

1. Chester Bernard maintains that authority will be accepted only under the following conditions:

   a. The individual can understand the order being communicated
   b. The individual believes the order is consistent with the purpose of the organization
   c. The individual sees the order as compatible with his or her personal interests
   d. The individual is mentally and physically able to comply with the order

D. Types of authority

1. **Line authority** – consists of the right to make decisions and to give orders concerning the production-, sales-, or finance-related behavior of subordinates.
2. **Staff authority** – consists of the right to advise or assist those who possess line authority

3. Line-Staff relationships

   a. Roles of Staff Personnel
      1. The advisory or counseling role
      2. The service role
      3. The control role

4. Conflict in Line-Staff Relationships

5. **Functional authority** – consists of the right to give orders within a segment of the management system in which the right is normally nonexistent

III. ACCOUNTABILITY

Accountability refers to the management philosophy whereby individuals are held liable, or accountable, for how well they use their authority or live up to their responsibility of performing predetermined activities.

IV. DELEGATION

Delegation is the process of aligning job activities and related authority to specific individuals in the organization.

A. Steps in Delegation Process

1. Assign specific duties to the individual
2. Grant appropriate authority to the subordinate
3. Create the obligation for the subordinate to perform the duties assigned

B. Obstacles to the Delegation Process

1. Obstacles related to the supervisor
2. Obstacles related to subordinates
3. Obstacles related to organizations

C. Eliminating Obstacles to the Delegation Process

1. Build subordinate confidence in the use of delegated authority
2. Minimize the impact of delegated authority on established working relationships
3. Help delegatees cope with problems whenever necessary

D. Centralization and Decentralization

1. **Centralization** – refers to the situation in which a minimal number of job activities and a minimal amount of authority are delegated to subordinates
2. **Decentralization** – refers to the situation in which a significant number of job activities and a maximum amount of authority are delegated to subordinates

E. Decentralizing an Organization: A Contingency Viewpoint

1. Specific questions managers can use to determine the amount of decentralization appropriate for a situation are as follows:

   a. What is the present size of the organization?
   b. Where are the organization's customers located?
   c. How homogeneous is the organization's product line?
   d. Where are organizational suppliers?
   e. Is there a need for quick decisions in the organization?
   f. Is creativity a desirable feature of the organization?

Chapter Eleven – Responsibility, Authority, and Delegation

    F. Decentralization at Massey-Ferguson: A Classic Example

        1. Guidelines for Decentralization

            a. The competence to make decisions must be possessed by the person to whom authority is delegated.
            b. Adequate and reliable information pertinent to the decision is required by the person making the decision.
            c. If a decision can be made by more than one unit of the enterprise, the authority to make the decision must rest with the manager accountable for the most units affected by the decision.

        2. Deregulation as a Frame of Mind
        3. Complementing Centralization
        4. Management Responsibilities

Test Your Knowledge

Essay

1. List and discuss the four outcomes that are possible when two or more employees are uncertain as to who is responsible for a task. (p. 238)

2. List and discuss five of the seven responsibility relationships among managers, as used in the management responsibility guide. (p. 239)

3. Discuss the four conditions under which authority will be accepted according to Chester Bernard. (p. 241)

4. Describe the three roles that staff personnel typically perform to assist line personnel. (p. 242)

5. List and discuss four of the six questions managers can use to determine the amount of decentralization appropriate for a situation. (p. 248)

True-False

T F   1. Responsibility is the obligation to perform assigned tasks. (p. 236)

T F   2. A job description specifies the level of education needed to perform a job. (p. 236)

T F   3. The functional similarity is the most complex model for dividing jobs. (p. 237)

T F   4. A responsibility gap exists when certain organizational tasks are not included in the responsibility area of any organizational member. (p. 238)

T F   5. Authority is the request to perform or order. (p. 240)

T F   6. Staff authority allows one to give orders. (p. 242)

T F   7. Accountability holds people liable for performance. (p. 244)

T F   8. Delegation is a process. (p. 245)

T F   9. When possible, managers delegate on the basis of employee interests. (p. 245)

Chapter Eleven – Responsibility, Authority, and Delegation

T F   10. Under centralization, subordinates have lots of authority. (p. 247)

Multiple Choice

1. Responsibility is the _____ to perform assigned activities. (p. 236)
   a. right
   b. responsibility
   c. obligation
   d. None are correct

2. A _____ is a listing of specific activities that must be performed to accomplish some task or job. (p. 236)
   a. job specification
   b. job description
   c. job analysis
   d. workflow analysis

3. What technology is changing the face of job hunting and job descriptions? (p. 237)
   a. computers
   b. Internet
   c. voice mail
   d. email

4. The _____ method is a method of dividing job activities in the organization. (p. 237)
   a. unity of command
   b. functional similarity
   c. empowerment
   d. delegation

5. _____ responsibility refers to a situation in which more than one individual is responsible for the same activity. (p. 238)
   a. Dysfunctional
   b. Functional
   c. Redundant
   d. Overlapping

6. A(n) _____ gap exists when certain organizational tasks are not included in the responsibility area of any individual organization member. (p. 238)
   a. overlapping
   b. compatibility
   c. command
   d. responsibility

7. The absence of clear, goal-oriented, nonoverlapping responsibilities undermines organizational _____. (p. 238)
   a. efficiency
   b. effectiveness
   c. procedures
   d. efficiency and effectiveness

8. A(n) _____ is a tool that is used to clarify the responsibilities of various managers in the organization. (p. 239)
   a. organizational chart
   b. Gantt chart
   c. management responsibility guide
   d. PERT chart

9. Which of the following best describes the concept of authority? (p. 240)
   a. the right to command
   b. the right to ask permission
   c. the obligation to try
   d. None are correct

10. _____ allows its holder to act in certain designated ways to directly influence the actions of others through orders. (p. 240)
    a. Responsibility
    b. Authority
    c. Coordination
    d. Compatibility

11. _____ consists of the right to make decisions and to give orders concerning the production-, sales-, or finance-related behavior of subordinates. (p. 241)
    a. Line authority
    b. Staff authority
    c. Unity of command
    d. Functional authority

12. What is the most fundamental authority in the organization? (p. 241)
    a. Staff
    b. Top management
    c. Line
    d. Functional

13. What is the role of staff personnel? (p. 242)
    a. Order
    b. Command
    c. Advise
    d. None are correct

14. In which of the following roles do staff personnel use their professional expertise to solve organizational problems? (p. 242)
    a. the advisory or counseling role
    b. the service role
    c. the control role
    d. the planning role

Chapter Eleven – Responsibility, Authority, and Delegation

15. Staff personnel help establish a mechanism for evaluating the effectiveness of organizational plans when using _____. (p. 243)
    a. the advisory or counseling role
    b. the service role
    c. the control role
    d. the planning role

16. _____ consists of the right to give orders within a segment of the management system in which the right is normally nonexistent. (p. 244)
    a. Line authority
    b. Staff authority
    c. Unity of command
    d. Functional authority

17. The process of assigning job activities and related authority to specific individuals in the organization is referred to as _____. (p. 245)
    a. unity of command
    b. delegation
    c. overlapping
    d. bureaucracy

18. _____ refers to the situation in which a minimal number of job activities and a minimal amount of authority are delegated to subordinates. (p. 247)
    a. Dysfunction
    b. Centralization
    c. Decentralization
    d. Boundaryless

19. The opposite of centralization is _____. (p. 247)
    a. Dysfunction
    b. Delegation
    c. Decentralization
    d. Boundaryless

20. _____ refers to the situation in which a significant number of job activities and a maximum amount of authority are delegated to subordinates. (p. 247)
    a. Dysfunction
    b. Delegation
    c. Decentralization
    d. Boundaryless

Fill-In

1. Managers can be described as _____ if they perform the activities they are obligated to perform (p. 239)

2. _____ allows its holder to allocate the organization's resources to achieve organizational objectives. (p. 240)

3. Practically speaking, _____ merely increases the probability that a specific command will be obeyed. (p. 240)

Chapter Eleven – Responsibility, Authority, and Delegation

4. _____ is the most fundamental authority within an organization. (p. 241)

5. Examples of organization members with _____ are people working in the accounting and human resource departments. (p. 242)

6. _____ is perhaps the most significant factor in determining whether or not an organization will have staff personnel. (p. 242)

7. In _____, staff personnel provide services that can more efficiently and effectively by provided by a single centralized staff group than by many individuals scattered throughout the organization. (p. 243)

8. The vice president of finance in an organization is an example of someone with _____ authority. (p. 244)

9. _____ refers to the management philosophy whereby individuals are held liable for how well they use their authority and live up to their responsibility of performing predetermined activities. (p. 244)

10. The situation in which a significant number of job activities and a maximum amount of authority are delegated to subordinates is referred to as _____. (p. 247)

Answers

Essay

1. The four outcomes that are possible when two or more employees are uncertain as to who is responsible for a task are:
    a. One of the two may perform the job. The other may either forget to or choose not do to the job—and neither of these is a desirable outcome for product quality control.
    b. Both employees may perform the job. Al the least, this results in duplicated effort, which dampens employee morale. At worst, one employee may diminish the value of the other employee's work, resulting in a decrement in product quality.
    c. Neither employee may perform the job because each assumed the other would do it.
    d. The employees may spend valuable time negotiating each aspect and phase of the job to carefully mesh their job responsibilities, thus minimizing both duplication of effort and responsibility gaps. Though time-consuming, this is actually the most desirable option in terms of product quality.

2. The seven responsibility relationships among managers, as used in the management responsibility guide are as follows:
    a. **General responsibility** – the individual who guides and directs the execution of ht function through the person accepting operating responsibility
    b. **Operating responsibility** – the individual who is directly responsible for the execution of the function
    c. **Specific responsibility** – the individual who is responsible for executing a specific or limited portion of the function
    d. **Must be consulted** – the individual whose area is affected by a decision who must be called on to render advice or relate information before any decision is made or approval is granted
    e. **May be consulted** – the individual who may be called on to relate information, render advice, or make recommendations before the action is taken
    f. **Must be notified** – the individual who must be notified of any action that has been taken

Chapter Eleven – Responsibility, Authority, and Delegation

g. **Must approve** – the individual (other than persons holding general and operating responsibility) who must approve or disapprove the decision

3. The four conditions under which authority will be accepted are as follows:
   a. The individual can understand the order being communicated
   b. The individual believes the order is consistent with the purpose of the organization
   c. The individual sees the order as compatible with his or her personal interests
   d. The individual is mentally and physically able to comply with the order

4. The roles that staff personnel typically perform to assist line personnel include:
   a. **The advisory or counseling role** – in this role, staff personnel use their professional expertise to solve organizational problems. The staff personnel are, in effect, internal consultants whose relationship with line personnel is similar to that of a professional and a client.
   b. **The service role** – staff personnel in this role provide services that can more efficiently and effectively be provided by a single centralized staff group than by many individuals scattered throughout the organization.
   c. **The control role** – in this role, staff personnel help establish a mechanism for evaluating the effectiveness of organizational plans. Staff personnel exercising this role are representatives, or agents, of top management.

5. The questions management can use to determine the amount of decentralization appropriate for a situation are as follows:
   a. **What is the present size of the organization?** – the larger the organization, the greater the likelihood that decentralization will be advantageous.
   b. **Where are the organization's customers located?** – as a general rule, the more physically separated the organization's customers are, the more viable a significant amount of decentralization is.
   c. **How homogeneous is the organization's product line?** – generally, as the product line becomes more heterogeneous, or diversified, the appropriateness of decentralization increases.
   d. **Where are organizational suppliers?** – time loss and high transportation costs associated with shipping raw materials over great distances from supplier to manufacturer could signal the need to decentralize certain functions.
   e. **Is there a need for quick decisions in the organization?** – if speedy decision making is essential, a considerable amount of decentralization is probably in order.
   f. **Is creativity a desirable feature of the organization?** – if creativity is desirable, then some decentralization is advisable, for decentralization allows delegatees the freedom to find better ways of doing things.

True-False

1. T	3. F	5. F	7. T	9. T
2. F	4. T	6. F	8. T	10. F

Multiple Choice

1. c	5. d	9. a	13. c	17. b
2. b	6. d	10. b	14. a	18. b
3. b	7. d	11. a	15. c	19. c
4. b	8. c	12. c	16. d	20. c

Chapter Eleven – Responsibility, Authority, and Delegation

Fill-In

1. responsible
2. Authority
3. authority
4. Line authority
5. staff authority
6. Size
7. the service role
8. functional
9. Accountability
10. decentralization

Modern Management (9th ed.)
Part 4 - Organizing
Chapter Twelve – Managing Human Resources

Overview

Human resources are essential to any organization and how these resources are managed in a firm is a critical element in a company's pathway to success. This chapter explores the various functions of human resources as well as developmental insight on testing and assessment centers. A discussion of the orientation and training process and performance appraisals is also provided in this chapter.

Chapter Outline

Introductory Case: Northwestern Mutual Life Focuses on Recruitment

I. DEFINING APPROPRIATE HUMAN RESOURCES

Appropriate human resources refers to the individuals within the organization who make a valuable contribution to management system goal attainment.

II. STEPS IN PROVIDING HUMAN RESOURCES

A. Recruitment

1. Recruitment is the initial attraction and screening of the supply of prospective human resources available to fill a position.

2. To be effective, recruiters must know the following:
   a. The job they are trying to fill
   b. Where potential human resources can be located
   c. How the low influences recruiting efforts

B. Knowing the Job

1. **Job analysis** – a technique commonly used to gain an understanding of what a task entails and the type of individual who should be hired to perform that task
2. **Job description** – a list of specific activities that must be performed to accomplish some task or job
3. **Job specification** – a list of the characteristics of the individual who should be hired to perform a specific task or job

C. Knowing Sources of Human Resources

1. Sources inside the organization

   a. **Human resource inventory** – an accumulation of information about the characteristics of organization members
   b. **Management inventory card** – contains the organizational history of an individual and indicates how that individual might be used in the organization in the future
   c. **Position replacement form** – summarizes information about organization members who could fill a position should it open up

Chapter Twelve – Managing Human Resources

        d. **Management manpower replacement chart** – is people oriented and presents a composite view of individuals management considers significant to human resource planning

    2. Sources Outside the Organization

        a. Competitors
        b. Employment agencies
        c. Readers of certain publications
        d. Educational institutions

  D. Knowing the Law

    1. **The Equal Employment Opportunity Commission** – an agency established to enforce federal laws prohibiting discrimination on the basis of race, color, religion, sex, and national origin in recruitment, hiring, firing, layoffs, and all other employment practices
    2. **Affirmative action** – organizational programs whose basic purpose is to eliminate barriers against, and increase employment opportunities for, underutilized or disadvantaged individuals.

III. SELECTION

  A. Selection is choosing an individual to hire from all those who have been recruited.

  B. Testing is examining human resources for qualities relevant to performing available jobs.

  C. Testing can be divided into four general categories:

    1. **Aptitude tests** – measures the potential of an individual to perform a task
    2. **Achievement tests** – measures the level of skill or knowledge an individual possesses in a certain area
    3. **Vocational interest tests** – attempt to measure an individual's interest in performing various kinds of jobs
    4. **Personality tests** – attempt to describe an individual's personality dimensions in such areas as emotional maturity, subjectivity, honesty, and objectivity

  D. Testing guidelines

    1. A test is **valid** if it measures what it is designed to measure.
    2. A test is **reliable** if it measures similarly time after time.

  E. Assessment center

An **assessment center** is a program (not a place) in which participants engage in a number of individual and group exercises constructed to stimulate important activities at the organizational levels to which they aspire.

IV. TRAINING

  A. Training is the process of developing qualities in human resources that will enable them to be more productive.

B. The training of individuals is essentially a four-step process:

1. Determining training needs
2. Designing the training program
3. Administering the training program
4. Evaluating the training program

C. Determining Training Needs

Training needs – the information or skill areas of an individual or group that require further development to increase the productivity of that individual or group

D. Designing the Training Program

F. Administering the Training Program

1. **Lectures** – a one-way communication situation in which an instructor trains an individual or group by orally presenting information
2. **Programmed learning** – a technique for instructing without the presence or intervention of a human instructor
3. **On-the-job-training** – a training technique that blends job-related knowledge with experience in using that knowledge on the job

F. Evaluating the Training Program

IV. PERFORMANCE APPRAISAL

A. Performance appraisal is the process of reviewing past productive activity to evaluate the contribution individuals have made toward attaining management system activities.

B. Why use performance appraisals?

1. They provide systematic judgments to support salary increases, promotions, transfers, and sometimes demotions or terminations.
2. They are a means of telling subordinates how they are doing and of suggesting needed changes in behavior, attitudes, skills, or job knowledge.
3. They furnish a useful basis for the coaching and counseling of individuals by superiors.

C. Handling performance appraisals

1. Performance appraisals should stress both performance in the position the individual holds and the success with which the individual is attaining organizational objectives.
2. Appraisals should emphasize how well the individual is doing the job, not the evaluator's impression of the individual's work habits.
3. The appraisal should be acceptable to both the evaluator and the subject

D. Potential weaknesses of performance appraisals

1. Performance appraisals focus employees on short-term rewards rather than on issues that are important to the long-run success of the organization.

2. Individuals involved in performance appraisals view them as a reward-punishment situation.
3. The emphasis of performance appraisal is on completing paperwork rather than on critiquing individual performance.
4. Individuals being evaluated view the process as unfair or biased.
5. Subordinates react negatively when evaluators offer unfavorable comments.

Test Your Knowledge

Essay

1. Define job analysis and discuss why the job analysis is important to the job description and job specification. (p. 259)

2. List and discuss the four primary advantages of hiring employees from competitors. (p. 262)

3. Define the purpose of the Equal Employment Opportunity Commission. (p. 263)

4. List and discuss the four categories of testing used in organizations for human resource selection. (p. 265)

5. List and discuss the two techniques used for transmitting information in training programs. (p. 269)

True-False

T F 1. Recruitment is a key factor at Northwestern Mutual Life. (p. 257)

T F 2. Appropriate human resources looks for valuable contributions of individuals. (p. 258)

T F 3. The first step in the human resources process is training. (p. 258)

T F 4. The second step in the human resource process is evaluation. (p. 258)

T F 5. The job specification is a list of characteristics of the individual who should be hired to perform a specific task or job. (p. 259)

T F 6. One of the sources of recruitment outside the organization is a competitor. (p. 262)

T F 7. The law has little influence on the recruiting process. (p. 263)

T F 8. Selection is dependent on recruitment. (p. 264)

T F 9. One type of human resources tests is a personality test. (p. 265)

T F 10. Performance appraisals serve as evaluation tools. (p. 271)

Multiple Choice

1. Northwestern Mutual Life is ranked where among insurance agencies in part due to its excellent human resources management? (p. 257)
   a. First
   b. Second
   c. Third
   d. Tenth

Chapter Twelve – Managing Human Resources

2. The second step in the human resources process is _____. (p. 258)
   a. Training
   b. Recruitment
   c. Selection
   d. Evaluation

3. _____ is a technique commonly used to gain an understanding of what a task entails and the type of individual who should be hired to perform that task. (p. 259)
   a. Job analysis
   b. Workflow diagram
   c. Work inventory
   d. Job description

4. In order to know the job, you must perform a(n) _____ (p. 259)
   a. job analysis
   b. workflow diagram
   c. work inventory
   d. job description

5. A(n) _____ is a list of specific activities that must be performed to accomplish some task or job. (p. 259)
   a. job analysis
   b. workflow diagram
   c. work inventory
   d. job description

6. One source of a pool of employees is inside the organization. Which of the following are means? (p. 260)
   a. Human resources inventory
   b. Management inventory card
   c. Position replacement form
   d. All are correct

7. The _____ is people oriented and presents a composite view of individuals that management considers significant to human resource planning. (p. 261)
   a. management inventory card
   b. position replacement form
   c. management manpower replacement chart
   d. job description

8. The EEOC stands for _____. (p. 263)
   a. Equal Employee Organization for Cooperation
   b. Equal Employer Opportunity Committee
   c. Equal Employment Opportunity Committee
   d. Equal Employment Opportunity Commission

9. If a company discriminates, what federal agency is likely to prosecute? (p. 263)
   a. Department of Justice
   b. Department of Labor
   c. Department of Affirmative Action
   d. EEOC

Chapter Twelve – Managing Human Resources

10. _____ is examining human resources for qualities relevant to performing available jobs. (p. 265)
    a. Testing
    b. Selecting
    c. Orientating
    d. Training

11. Tests that measure the level of skill or knowledge an individual possesses in a certain area are called _____. (p. 265)
    a. aptitude tests
    b. achievement tests
    c. vocational interest tests
    d. personality tests

12. Which of the following are types of tests? (p. 265)
    a. Aptitude
    b. Achievement
    c. Vocational interest
    d. All are correct

13. An assessment center is a(n) _____. (p. 266)
    a. place
    b. degree
    c. program
    d. None are correct

14. A program in which participants engage in, and are evaluated on, a number of individual and group exercises constructed to simulate important activities at the organizational levels to which they aspire is called a(n)_____. (p. 266)
    a. assessment center
    b. achievement center
    c. personality evaluation
    d. orientation program

15. _____ is the process of developing qualities in human resources that will enable them to be more productive. (p. 267)
    a. Orienting
    b. Training
    c. Evaluating
    d. Selecting

16. The information or skill areas of an individual or group that require further development to increase the productivity of that individual or group are called _____. (p. 268)
    a. assessment needs
    b. personality needs
    c. training needs
    d. orienting needs

Chapter Twelve – Managing Human Resources

17. A(n) _____ is primarily a one-way communication situation in which an instructor trains an individual or group by orally presenting information. (p. 269)
    a. lecture
    b. management game
    c. role play
    d. position rotation

18. A training technique for instructing without the presence or intervention of a human instructor is called _____. (p. 269)
    a. programmed learning
    b. television
    c. tapes
    d. None are correct

19. _____ is a training technique that blends job-related knowledge with experience in using that knowledge at the job. (p. 270)
    a. Programmed learning
    b. A lecture
    c. On-the-job-training
    d. Scenario analysis

20. The process of reviewing past productive activity to evaluate the contribution individuals have made toward attaining management system objectives is called _____. (p. 271)
    a. orientation
    b. performance appraisal
    c. selection
    d. recruitment

Fill-In

1. _____ is the initial attraction and screening of the supply of prospective human resources available to fill a position. (p. 259)

2. The _____ contains the organizational history of an individual and indicates how that individual might be used in the organization in the future. (p. 261)

3. The _____ summarizes information about organization members who could fill a position should it open up. (p. 261)

4. The agency established to enforce federal laws regulating recruiting and other employment practices is called the _____. (p. 263)

5. _____ are organizational programs whose basic purpose is to eliminate barriers against and increase employment opportunities for underutilized or disadvantaged individuals. (p. 264)

6. A test is _____ if it measures what it is designed to measure. (p. 265)

7. If a test measures similarly time after time, it is considered to be _____. (p. 265)

8. _____ is direct scrutinizing of how well an individual is performing a job. (p. 270)

9. The most common format for _____ requires small groups of trainees to (p. 270)
   make and then evaluate various management decisions.

10. _____ involves moving an individual from job to job to enable the person (p. 270)
    to gain an understanding of the organization as a whole.

Answers

Essay

1. Recruitment activities must begin with a thorough understanding of the position to be filled so the broad range of potential employees can be narrowed down intelligently. The technique commonly used to gain that understanding is known as **job analysis.** Basically, job analysis is aimed at determining a **job description** (the activities a job entails) and a **job specification** (the characteristics of the individual who should be hired for the job).

2. The four primary advantages of hiring from competitors include:
   a. The individual knows the business
   b. The competitor will have paid for the individual's training up to the time of hire
   c. The competing organization will probably be weakened somewhat by the loss of the individual
   d. Once hired, the individual will be a valuable source of information about how to best compete with the other organization

3. The **Equal Employment Opportunity Commission (EEOC)** is an agency established to enforce federal laws prohibiting discrimination on the basis of race, color, religion, sex, and national origin in recruitment, hiring, firing, layoffs, and all other employment practices. Equal opportunity legislation protects the right of a citizen to work and obtain a fair wage based primarily on merit and performance.

4. The four categories of organizational testing include:
   a. **Aptitude tests** – tests of aptitude measure the potential of an individual to perform a task
   b. **Achievement test** – tests that measure the level of skill or knowledge an individual possesses in a certain area
   c. **Vocational interest tests** – test of vocational interest attempt to measure an individual's interest in performing various kinds of jobs
   d. **Personality tests** – these tests attempt to describe an individual's personality dimensions in such areas as emotional maturity, subjectivity, honesty, and objectivity

5. The two techniques used for transmitting information in training programs are:
   a. **Lectures** – primarily a one-way communication situation in which an instructor trains an individual or group by orally presenting information. This is perhaps the most widely used technique for transmitting information in training programs.
   b. **Programmed learning** – a technique for instructing without the presence or intervention of a human instructor. Small pieces of information requiring responses are presented to individual trainees, and the trainees determine from checking their responses against provided answers whether their understanding of the information is accurate.

True-False

1. T
2. T
3. F
4. F
5. T
6. T
7. F
8. T
9. T
10. T

Multiple Choice

1. a
2. c
3. a
4. a
5. d
6. d
7. c
8. d
9. d
10. a
11. b
12. d
13. c
14. a
15. b
16. c
17. a
18. a
19. c
20. b

Fill-In

1. Recruitment
2. management inventory card
3. position replacement form
4. Equal Employment Opportunity Commission
5. Affirmative action programs
6. valid
7. reliable
8. Coaching
9. management games
10. Position rotation

Modern Management (9th ed.)
Part 4 - Organizing
Chapter Thirteen – Organizational Change and Stress

Overview

Change has always been part and parcel of organizations. This chapter introduces the variety of changes that are happening in the world. It presents the importance of stability, how organizations can try to recognize change, and how people are impacted by change, as well as an evaluation of change.

Chapter Outline

Introductory Case: AT&T Changes Where and How People Work

I. FUNDAMENTALS OF CHANGING AN ORGANIZATION

    A. Defining "Changing an Organization"

        1. Changing an organization is the process of modifying an existing organization to increase organizational effectiveness.

        2. The Importance of Change

            a. Most managers agree that if an organization is to thrive, it must change continually in response to significant development in the environment, such as changing customer needs, technological breakthroughs, and new government regulations.

    B. Change versus Stability

II. FACTORS TO CONSIDER WHEN CHANGING AN ORGANIZATION

    A. The Change Agent

    A **change agent** is an individual inside or outside the organization who tries to modify an existing organizational situation.

    B. Determining What Should be Changed

        1. **People factors** – attitudes, leadership skills, communication skills, and all other characteristics of the organization's employees
        2. **Structural factors** – organizational controls such as policies and procedures
        3. **Technological factors** – any types of equipment or processes that assist organization members in the performance of their jobs

    C. The Kind of Change to Make

        1. **Technological change** – a type of organizational change that emphasizes modifying the level of technology in the management system
        2. **Structural change** – a type of organizational change that emphasizes modifying an existing organization structure

            a. **Matrix organization** – a traditional organizational structure that is modified primarily for the purpose of completing some kind of special project

3. **People Change** – a type of organizational change that emphasizes modifying certain aspects of organization members to increase organizational effectiveness

   a. Describing People Change—Organizational Development (OD)

      1. OD is a process the focuses on changing organizational members
      2. Grid organizational development is a commonly used organization development technique based on a theoretical model call the managerial grid
      3. A managerial grid is a theoretical model based on the premise that concern for people and concern for production are the two primary attitudes the influence management style
      4. The status of OD – OD techniques are currently being applied not only to business organizations but also to many other types of organizations, such as religious organizations

D. Individuals Affected by the Change

   1. Resistance to change within an organization is as common as the need for change.

   2. Reducing resistance to change can be accomplished by following the guidelines below:

      a. Avoid surprises – whenever possible, individuals who will be affected by a change should be informed of the kind of change being considered and the probability that it will be adopted
      b. Promote real understanding – when fear of personal loss related to a proposed change is reduced, opposition to the change is also reduced
      c. Set the stage for change – perhaps the most powerful tool for reducing resistance to change is management's positive attitude toward the change
      d. Make tentative change – tentative change is based on the assumption that a trial period during which organization members live under a change is the best way of reducing feared personal loss.

E. Evaluation of Change - managers should spend time evaluating the changes they make

III. CHANGE AND STRESS

   A. Defining Stress

   Stress is the bodily strain that an individual experiences as a result of coping with some environmental factor.

   B. The Importance of Studying Stress

      1. Stress can have damaging psychological and physiological effects on employees' health and on their contributions to organizational effectiveness.
      2. Stress is a major cause of employee absenteeism and turnover.
      3. A stressed employee can affect the safety of other workers or even the public.
      4. Stress represents a very significant cost to organizations.

   C. Managing Stress In Organizations

1. Understanding how stress influences worker performance
2. Identifying unhealthy stress in organizations
3. Helping employees handle stress
4. Reducing stressors in the organization

   a. Create an organizational climate the is supportive of individuals
   b. Make jobs interesting
   c. Design and operate career counseling programs

IV. VIRTUALITY

   A. Defining the Virtual Organization

   A **virtual organization** is an organization having the essence of a traditional organization but without some aspects of traditional boundaries and structures.

   B. Degrees of Virtuality

   1. **Virtual organization** – an organization having the essence of a traditional organization, but without some aspect of traditional boundaries and structure
   2. **Virtual corporation** – an organization that goes significantly beyond the boundaries and structure of a traditional organization
   3. **Virtual teams** – groups of employees formed by managers that go beyond the boundaries and structure of traditional teams
   4. **Virtual training** – a training process that goes beyond the boundaries and structure of traditional training

   C. The Virtual Office

   1. A virtual office is a work arrangement that extends beyond the structure and boundaries of the traditional office arrangement.

      a. Occasional telecommuting
      b. Hoteling
      c. Tethered in office
      d. Home-based, some mobility
      e. Fully mobile

   D. Reasons for Establishing a Virtual Office

   1. Cost reduction
   2. Increase productivity
   3. Redesigning jobs

   E. Challenges to Managing a Virtual Office

   1. Virtual offices make it more difficult to build desired corporate culture.
   2. Virtual offices make it more difficult for managers to control workers.
   3. Virtual offices make communication more difficult.

Chapter Thirteen – Organizational Change and Stress

Test Your Knowledge

Essay

1. List and discuss the three classes of factors on which the activities of organizational effectiveness depend. (p. 283)

2. List five specific weaknesses that are commonly voiced in the efforts of organizational development. (p. 289)

3. Discuss four specific guidelines that can be used to reduce resistance to change. (p. 290)

4. List four specific reasons why studying stress is important. (p. 291)

5. Discuss three strategies that management can adopt to help prevent the initial development of unwanted stressors in organizations. (p. 293)

True-False

T F 1. AT&T's AWAs are team focused. (p. 279)

T F 2. Organizations change to increase effectiveness. (p. 280)

T F 3. A change agent can only come from outside the organization. (p. 282)

T F 4. One of the major people factors in change is attitude. (p. 283)

T F 5. Structural factors in change include equipment. (p. 283)

T F 6. OD stands for organizational design for change. (p. 287)

T F 7. A managerial grid is a hands-on practical guide to managing. (p. 287)

T F 8. Luckily, the effectiveness of OD programs is easy to measure and evaluate. (p. 288)

T F 9. The resistance to change is as common as the need for change. (p. 289)

T F 10. The most extensive degree of Virtuality is the virtual corporation. (p. 294)

Multiple Choice

1. A(n) _____ is an individual inside or outside the organization who tries to modify an existing organizational situation. (p. 282)
   a. whistle blower
   b. change agent
   c. team leader
   d. manager

Chapter Thirteen – Organizational Change and Stress

2. _____ are attitudes, leadership skills, communication skills, and all other characteristics of the organization's employees. (p. 283)
   a. People factors
   b. Structural factors
   c. Technological factors
   d. Environmental factors

3. Organizational controls such as policies and procedures are called _____. (p. 283)
   a. people factors
   b. structural factors
   c. technological factors
   d. environmental factors

4. _____ are any types of equipment or processes that assist organization members in the performance of their jobs. (p. 283)
   a. People factors
   b. Structural factors
   c. Technological factors
   d. Environmental factors

5. Change can affect which of the following? (p. 283)
   a. Technology
   b. People
   c. Structure
   d. All are correct

6. _____ is a type of organizational change that emphasizes modifying the level of technology in the management system. (p. 284)
   a. Technological change
   b. Structural change
   c. People change
   d. Environmental change

7. A type of organizational change that emphasizes modifying an organizational structure is called _____. (p. 284)
   a. technological change
   b. structural change
   c. people change
   d. environmental change

8. A(n) _____ organization is a traditional organizational structure that is modified primarily for the purpose of completing some kind of special project. (p. 285)
   a. functional
   b. product
   c. customer
   d. matrix

Chapter Thirteen – Organizational Change and Stress

9. _____ is a type of organizational change that emphasizes modifying certain aspects of organization members to increase organizational effectiveness. (p. 287)
   a. Technological change
   b. Structural change
   c. People change
   d. Environmental change

10. The process that emphasizes changing an organization by changing organization members and bases these changes on an overview of structure, technology, and all other organizational ingredients is called _____. (p. 287)
    a. organizational dynamics
    b. organizational development
    c. organizational design
    d. None are correct

11. In terms of change, OD stands for what? (p. 287)
    a. organizational dynamics
    b. organizational development
    c. organizational design
    d. None are correct

12. A(n) _____ is a theoretical model based on the premise that concern for people and concern for production are the two primary attitudes that influence management style. (p. 287)
    a. correlation chart
    b. perceptual map
    c. managerial grid
    d. manpower chart

13. Which of the following is NOT a theoretical axis of the managerial grid? (p. 288)
    a. Concern for people
    b. Concern for profit
    c. Concern for production
    d. All are featured in the managerial grid.

14. Which among the following are ways to reduce resistance to change? (p. 290)
    a. Avoid surprises
    b. Promote real understanding
    c. Set the stage for change
    d. All are correct

15. What is considered the bodily strain that an individual experiences as a result of coping with some environmental factor? (p. 291)
    a. Stress
    b. Change
    c. Development
    d. None are correct

Chapter Thirteen – Organizational Change and Stress

16. Virtual organizations are also referred to as what? (p. 294)
    a. Network
    b. Modular
    c. Bureaucratic
    d. Both a & b

17. A(n) _____ organization is an organization having the essence of a traditional organization, but without some aspect of traditional boundaries and structure. (p. 294)
    a. virtual
    b. mechanistic
    c. organic
    d. transmodal

18. The most extensive degree of Virtuality is what? (p. 294)
    a. Virtual reality
    b. Virtual corporation
    c. Virtual team
    d. Virtual person

19. _____ are groups of employees formed by managers that go beyond the boundaries and structure of traditional teams. (p. 295)
    a. Matrix teams
    b. Programmed teams
    c. Mechanistic teams
    d. Virtual teams

20. A work arrangement that extends beyond the structure and boundaries of the traditional office arrangement is called _____. (p. 295)
    a. a virtual team
    b. programmed learning
    c. a virtual office
    d. coordinating

Fill-In

1. _____ emphasizes modifying the level of technology in the management system. (p. 284)

2. _____ emphasizes increasing organizational effectiveness by changing controls that influence organization members during the performance of their jobs. (p. 284)

3. Matrix organizations are also called _____. (p. 285)

4. Grid organization development is a commonly used organization development technique based on a theoretical model called the _____. (p. 287)

5. The bodily strain that an individual experiences as a result of coping with some environmental factor is _____. (p. 291)

Chapter Thirteen – Organizational Change and Stress

6. A(n) _____ is an environmental demand that causes people to feel stress. (p. 293)

7. _____ are also referred to as network organizations or modular organizations. (p. 294)

8. _____ is a training process that goes beyond the boundaries and structure of traditional training. (p. 295)

9. A work arrangement that extends beyond the structure and boundaries of the traditional office arrangement is called a(n) _____. (p. 295)

10. _____ is the most commonly cited reason managers design and implement virtual offices. (p. 296)

Answers

Essays

1. The three classes of factors are as follows:
    a. **People factors** – attitudes, leadership skills, communication skills, and other characteristics of the organization's employees
    b. **Structural factors** – organizational control such as policies and procedures
    c. **Technological factors** – any types of equipment or processes that assist organization members in the performance of jobs

2. The five weaknesses commonly voiced in the efforts of organizational development (OD) include:
    a. The effectiveness of an OD program is difficult to evaluate
    b. OD programs are generally too time-consuming
    c. OD objectives are commonly too vague
    d. The total costs of an OD program are difficult to gauge at the time the program starts
    e. OD programs are generally too expensive

3. The four guidelines to reducing resistance to change include:
    a. **Avoid surprises** – whenever possible, individuals who will be affected by a change should be informed of the kind of change being considered and the probability that it will be adopted
    b. **Promote real understanding** – when fear of personal loss related to a proposed change is reduced, opposition to the change is also reduced
    c. **Set the stage for change** – management should convey that change is one of the basic prerequisites for a successful organization
    d. **Make tentative change** – this approach establishes a trial period during which organization members spend some time working under a proposed change before voicing support nonsupport of it

4. The four reasons why studying stress is important are:
    a. Stress can have damaging psychological and physiological effects on employees' health and on their contributions to organizational effectiveness.
    b. Stress is a major cause of employee absenteeism and turnover.
    c. A stressed employee can affect the safety of other workers or even the public.
    d. Stress represents a very significant cost to organizations.

Chapter Thirteen – Organizational Change and Stress

5. <u>The three strategies that can be used to help prevent the initial development of unwanted stressors include:</u>
   a. Create an organizational climate that is supportive of individuals – organizations commonly evolve into large bureaucracies with formal, inflexible, impersonal climates. This setup leads to considerable job stress. Making the organizational environment less formal and more supportive of employee needs will help prevent the development of unwanted organizational stressors.
   b. Make jobs interesting – routine jobs that do not allow employees some degree of freedom often result in undesirable employee stress. If management focuses on making jobs as interesting as possible, this should help prevent the development of stressors related to routine, boring jobs.
   c. Design and operate career counseling programs – employees often experience considerable stress when they do not know what their next career step might be or when they might take it. If management can show employees that next step and when it can realistically be achieved, it will discourage unwanted organizational stressors in this area.

True-False

1. T	3. F	5. F	7. F	9. T
2. T	4. T	6. F	8. F	10. T

Multiple Choice

1. b	5. d	9. c	13. b	17. a
2. a	6. a	10. b	14. d	18. b
3. b	7. b	11. b	15. d	19. d
4. c	8. d	12. c	16. d	20. c

Fill-In

1. Technological change
2. Structural change
3. project organizations
4. managerial grid
5. stress
6. stressor
7. Virtual organizations
8. Virtual training
9. virtual office
10. Cost reduction

Modern Management (9th ed.)
Part 5 - Influencing
Chapter Fourteen – Fundamentals of Influencing and Communication

Overview

This chapter covers the concept of influencing and interpersonal communications. Also presented are the areas of feedback, nonverbal communications, and formal organizational communications. There is a focus on the grapevine and the importance of its role, as well as some hints on how to improve organizational communication.

Chapter Outline

Introductory Case: Eaton Managers Concentrate on Influencing People

I. FUNDAMENTALS OF INFLUENCING

　A. Defining influencing

　　Influencing is the process of guiding the activities of the organization members in appropriate directions involving the performance of four management activities: leading, motivating, considering groups, and communicating.

　B. The influencing subsystem—input, process, and output

　　1. Leading
　　2. Motivating
　　3. Considering groups
　　4. Communicating

II. COMMUNICATION

　A. **Communication** is the process of sharing information with other individuals.

　B. Interpersonal communication

　　1. How interpersonal communication works

　　　a. Source/encoder
　　　b. Message
　　　c. Signal
　　　d. Decoder/destination.

　　2. Successful and Unsuccessful Interpersonal Communication

　　　a. **Successful communication** refers to an interpersonal communication situation in which the information the source intends to share with the destination and the meaning the destination derives from the transmitted message are the same.
　　　b. **Unsuccessful communication** is an interpersonal communication situation in which the information the source intends to share with the destination and the meaning the destination derives from the transmitted message are different.

3. Barriers to Successful Interpersonal Communications

   a. **Macrobarriers** – factors hindering successful communication that relate primarily to the communication environment and the larger world in which communication takes place

      1. The increasing need for information
      2. The need for increasingly complex information
      3. The reality that people in the U.S. are increasingly coming into contact with people who use languages other than English
      4. The constant need to learn new concepts cuts down on the time available for communication

   b. **Microbarriers** – factors hindering successful communication that relate primarily to such variables as the communication message, the source, and the destination

      1. The source's view of the destination
      2. Message interference
      3. The destination's view of the source
      4. Perception
      5. Multimeaning words

4. Feedback and Interpersonal Communication

   Feedback is the interpersonal communication situation – the destination's reaction to a message.

5. Achieving Communication Effectiveness

   a. Seek to clarify ideas before communicating
   b. Examine the true purpose of each communication
   c. Consider the total physical and human setting whenever communicating
   d. Consult with others, when appropriate, in planning communications
   e. Be mindful of the overtones while communicating rather than merely the basic content of the message
   f. Take the opportunity, when it arises, to convey something of help or value to the receiver
   g. Follow up the communication
   h. Communicate for tomorrow as well as today
   i. Be sure the actions support the communication
   j. Seek not only to be understood, but also to understand

6. Verbal and Nonverbal Interpersonal Communications

   a. **Verbal communication** is the sharing of information through words, either written or spoken.
   b. **Nonverbal communications** is the sharing of information without using words.

C. Interpersonal Communication in Organizations

1. **Organizational communication** is defined as interpersonal communications within organizations.
2. Formal Organizational Communication

    a. Types of formal organizational communication

    1. **Downward organizational communication** – communication that flows from any point on an organization chart downward to another point on the organization chart
    2. **Upward organizational communication** – communication that flows from any point on an organization chart upward to another point on the organization chart
    3. **Lateral organizational communication** – communication that flows from any point on an organization chart horizontally to another point on the organization chart

3. Patterns of Formal Organizational Communication

    a. **Serial transmission** – involves the passing of information from one individual to another in a series

4. Informal Organizational Communication

    a. Informal organizational communication is organizational communication that does not follow the lines of the organizational chart.
    b. The **grapevine** is the network of informal organizational communication.
    c. Three main characteristics of the grapevine:

        1. It springs up and is used irregularly within the organization.
        2. It is not controlled by top executives, who may not even be able to influence it.
        3. It exists largely to serve the self-interests of the people within it.

Test Your Knowledge

Essay

1. List and discuss the three basic elements that make the interpersonal communication process complete. (p. 308)

2. Define communication macrobarriers and list four common communication macrobarriers. (p. 309)

3. List and discuss the five common communication microbarriers. (p. 309)

4. Define formal organizational communication and discuss the three basic types of formal organizational communication. (p. 314)

5. Define the grapevine and list three main characteristics of the grapevine. (p. 317)

Chapter Fourteen – Fundamentals of Influencing and Communication

True-False

T F 1. Teams are used for communicating at Eaton. (p. 303)

T F 2. The act of influencing is a process of guiding events. (p. 304)

T F 3. The influencing process includes motivating. (p. 304)

T F 4. Input entails customers and competitors. (p. 306)

T F 5. Communication is a one-way transmission. (p. 307)

T F 6. A common microbarrier in communications is message interference. (p. 309)

T F 7. Perception is the interpretation of the message by an individual. (p. 310)

T F 8. Feedback is a reaction to a message in terms of communications. (p. 311)

T F 9. One means of achieving effective communications is to seek to clarify your ideas before communicating. (p. 312)

T F 10. Serial transmission is a type of informal communication. (p. 316)

Multiple Choice

1. Influencing involves all of the following management activities EXCEPT: (p. 304)
   a. Leading
   b. Controlling
   c. Motivating
   d. Communicating

2. Input entails which of the following? (p. 306)
   a. People
   b. Money
   c. Raw materials
   d. All are correct

3. Communication is a(n) _____. (p. 306)
   a. process
   b. function
   c. objective
   d. None are correct

4. What is the #1 skill that chief executives believe should be taught to management students? (p. 307)
   a. Financial management
   b. Interpersonal skills
   c. Oral and written skills
   d. Understanding economics

Chapter Fourteen – Fundamentals of Influencing and Communication

5. The _____ is the person in the interpersonal communication situation who originates and encodes information to be shared with another person or persons. (p. 308)
    a. source
    b. signal
    c. decoder
    d. destination

6. The person or persons in the interpersonal communication situation with whom the source is attempting to share information is called the _____. (p. 308)
    a. encoder
    b. source
    c. signal
    d. destination

7. A message is _____ information that the source intends to share with others. (p. 308)
    a. signal
    b. encoded
    c. transmittal
    d. None are correct

8. Which of the following are macrobarriers to communication? (p. 308)
    a. Increasing need for information
    b. Need for increasingly complex information
    c. The constant need to learn new concepts
    d. All are correct

9. The interpretation of a message by an individual is called _____. (p. 310)
    a. reality
    b. communication
    c. decoder
    d. perception

10. _____ communication is the sharing of information through words, either written or spoken. (p. 313)
    a. Transitional
    b. Nonverbal
    c. Virtual
    d. Verbal

11. Communication without the use of words is called _____ communication. (p. 313)
    a. transitional
    b. nonverbal
    c. virtual
    d. None are correct

12. _____ communication is interpersonal communication within organizations. (p. 314)
    a. Transitional
    b. Virtual
    c. Organizational
    d. Hybrid

Chapter Fourteen – Fundamentals of Influencing and Communication

13. Organizational communication that follows the lines of the organization chart is called _____ communication. (p. 314)
    a. informal
    b. formal
    c. transitional
    d. task-oriented

14. _____ organizational communication is communication that flows from any point on an organization chart downward to another point on the organization chart. (p. 314)
    a. Downward
    b. Upward
    c. Lateral
    d. Transitional

15. Which of the following is NOT one of the three basic types of formal organizational communication? (p. 314)
    a. downward
    b. upward
    c. lateral
    d. transitional

16. Organizational communication that contains primarily the information managers need to evaluate the organizational area for which they are responsible and to determine if something is going wrong within it is called _____ organizational communication. (p. 315)
    a. downward
    b. upward
    c. lateral
    d. transitional

17. _____ organizational communication is communication that flows from any point on an organization chart horizontally to another point on the organization chart. (p. 315)
    a. Downward
    b. Upward
    c. Lateral
    d. Transitional

18. What type of transmission involves the passing of information from one individual to another in a series? (p. 316)
    a. Consequential
    b. Various
    c. Serial
    d. None are correct

19. _____ organizational communication is organizational communication that does not follow the lines of the organization chart. (p. 317)
    a. Downward
    b. Upward
    c. Informal
    d. Transitional

Chapter Fourteen – Fundamentals of Influencing and Communication

20. The network of information organizational communication is referred to as the _____ (p. 317)
    a. Informal lines
    b. Grapevine
    c. New wave tech
    d. None are correct

Fill-In

1. The _____ is a message that has been transmitted from one person to another. (p. 308)

2. Communication _____ are factors that hinder successful communication in a general communication situation. (p. 309)

3. Factors that hinder successful communication in a specific communication situation are called communication _____. (p. 309)

4. _____ refers to stimuli that compete with the communication message for the attention of the destination. (p. 310)

5. _____ is the interpersonal communication situation, the destination's reaction to a message. (p. 311)

6. The sharing of information without using words is called _____ communication. (p. 313)

7. _____ relates primarily to the direction and control of employees. (p. 314)

8. Techniques that managers commonly use to encourage _____ organizational communication are informal discussions with employees and attitude surveys. (p. 315)

9. _____ is communication that flows across the organization usually focusing on coordinating the activities of various departments and developing new plans for future operating periods. (p. 315)

10. A(n) _____ involves the passing of information from one individual to another in a series. (p. 316)

Answers

Essay

1. The three basic elements of the interpersonal communication process are as follows:
    a. **The source/encoder** – the person in the interpersonal communication situation who originates and encodes information to be shared with others
    b. **The signal** – encoded information that the source intends to share
    c. **The decoder/destination** – the person with whom the source is attempting to share information

2. **Communication macrobarriers** are factors that hinder successful communication in a general communication situation. These factors relate primarily to the communication environment and the larger world in which communication takes place. The four common communication microbarriers are:
    a. The increasing need for information
    b. The need for increasingly complex information
    c. The reality that people in the U.S. are increasingly coming into contact with people who use languages other than English
    d. The constant need to learn new concepts cuts down on the time available for communication

Chapter Fourteen – Fundamentals of Influencing and Communication

3. The five common communication microbarriers include the following:
    a. **The source's view of the destination** – the source in any communication situation has a tendency to view the destination in a specifc way, and this view influences the messages sent
    b. **Message interference** – stimuli that compete with the communication message for the attention of the destination
    c. **The destination's view of the source** – certain attitudes of the destination toward the source can also hinder successful communication
    d. **Perception** – an individuals interpretation of a message
    e. **Multimeaning words** – because many words in the English language have several meanings, a destination may have difficulty deciding which meaning should be attached to the words of a meaning

4. **Formal organizational communication** is organizational communication that follows the lines of the organization chart. The three basic types of formal organizational communication include:
    a. **Downward organizational communication** – communication that flows from any point on an organization chart to another point on the organization chart
    b. **Upward organizational communication** – communication that flows from any point on an organization chart upward to another point on the organization chart
    c. **Lateral organizational communication** – communication that flows from any point on an organization chart horizontally to another point on the organization chart

5. The **grapevine** is the network of informal organizational communication that has the following three main characteristics:
    a. It springs up and is used irregularly within the organization.
    b. It is not controlled by top executives, who may not even be able to influence it.
    c. It exists largely to serve the self-interests of the people within it.

True-False

1. T
2. T
3. T
4. F
5. F
6. F
7. T
8. T
9. T
10. F

Multiple Choice

1. b
2. d
3. a
4. c
5. a
6. d
7. b
8. d
9. d
10. d
11. b
12. c
13. b
14. a
15. d
16. b
17. c
18. c
19. c
20. b

Fill-In

1. signal
2. macrobarriers
3. microbarriers
4. Message interference
5. Feedback
6. nonverbal
7. Downward organizational communication
8. upward organizational communication
9. Lateral organizational communication
10. serial transmission

Modern Management (9th ed.)
Part 5 - Influencing
Chapter Fifteen - Leadership

Overview

This chapter presents a working definition of leadership, and also includes information about the trait and situational approaches to leadership. Leadership theories that focus on more general organizational situations are also covered. Also included is a discussion of alternatives to leader flexibility and an appreciation for emerging leadership styles and issues today.

Chapter Outline

Introductory Case: The President of H.J. Heinz Company Sends a Letter

I. DEFINING LEADERSHIP

    1. **Leadership** is the process of directing the behavior of others toward the accomplishment of objectives.
    2. Leading is not the same as managing.

II. THE TRAIT THEORY OF LEADERSHIP

    A. The **trait approach to leadership** is an outdated view of leadership that sees the personal characteristics of an individual as the main determinants of how successful that individual could be as a leader.

    B. Successful leaders tend to possess the following characteristics:

       1. Intelligence, including judgment and verbal ability
       2. Past achievement in scholarship and athletics
       3. Emotional maturity and stability
       4. Dependability, persistence, and a drive for continuing achievement
       5. The skill to participate socially and adapt to various groups
       6. A desire for status and socioeconomic position

III. THE SITUATIONAL THEORY OF LEADERSHIP: A FOCUS ON LEADER BEHAVIOR

    A. **The situational approach to leadership** is a relatively modern view of leadership that suggests that successful leadership requires a unique combination of leaders, followers, and leadership situations.

    B. Leadership Situations and Decisions

       1. The Tannenbaum and Schmidt Leadership Continuum

          a. The manager makes the decision and announces it
          b. The manager "sells" the decision
          c. The manager presents ideas and invites questions
          d. The manager presents a tentative decision that is subject to change
          e. The manager presents the problem, gets suggestions, and then makes the decision
          f. The manager defines the limits and asks the group to make a decision
          g. The manager permits the group to make decisions within prescribed limits

2. Determining How to Make Decisions as a Leader

   a. Forces in the manager
   b. Forces in the subordinate
   c. Forces in the situation

3. Determining How to Make Decisions as a Leader: An Update

   The update pointed out that new organizational environments had to be considered in determining how to lead.

4. The Vroom-Yetton-Jago Model (VYJ Model)

   a. Two important premises of the VYJ model

      1. Organizational decisions should be of high quality
      2. Subordinates should accept and be committed to organizational decisions that are made

C. Leadership Behaviors

   1. The OSU Studies

      a. **Structure behavior** – leadership activity that delineates the relationship between the leader and the leader's followers or establishes well-defined procedures that followers should adhere to in performing the jobs
      b. **Consideration behavior** – leadership behavior that reflects friendship, mutual trust, respect, and warmth in the relationship between leader and followers
      c. **Leadership style** – the behavior a leader exhibits when guiding organizational members in appropriate directions

   2. Michigan Studies

      a. **Job-centered behavior** – leader behavior that focuses primarily on the work a subordinate is doing
      b. **Employee-centered behavior** – leader behavior that focuses primarily on subordinates as people

   3. Effectiveness of Various Leadership Styles

      Leadership situations are so varied that pronouncing one leadership style as the most effective is an oversimplification.

   4. The Hersey-Blanchard Life Cycle Theory of Leadership

      The **life cycle theory of leadership** is a leadership concept that hypothesizes that leadership styles should reflect primarily the maturity level of the followers.

5. Fiedler's Contingency Theory

    a. **Leader flexibility** – the ability to change leadership style
    b. The **contingency theory of leadership** is a leadership concept that hypothesizes that, in any given leadership situation, leader-member relations, task structure, and the position power of the leader are the three primary factors that should be considered when moving leaders into situations appropriate for their leadership styles.

6. The Path-Goal Theory of Leadership

    a. **The path-goal theory of leadership** suggests that the primary activities of a leader are to make desirable and achievable rewards available to organization members who attain organizational goals and to clarify the kinds of behavior that must be performed to earn those rewards.

    b. Four primary types of behavior according to the path-goal theory of leadership:

        1. Directive behavior
        2. Supportive behavior
        3. Participative behavior
        4. Achievement behavior

IV. LEADERSHIP TODAY

A. **Transformational Leadership**—leadership that inspires organizational success by profoundly affecting followers' beliefs in what an organization should be, as well as their values, such as justice and integrity

    1. The tasks of transformational leaders

        a. Raise followers' awareness of organizational issues and their consequences
        b. Create a vision of what the organization should be, build commitment to that vision throughout the organization, and facilitate organizational changes that support the vision

B. **Coaching**—leadership that instructs followers on how to meet the special organizational challenges they face

    1. Coaching behavior

        a. Listens closely
        b. Gives emotional support
        c. Shows by example what constitutes appropriate behavior

C. **Superleadership**—leadership that inspires organizational success by showing followers how to lead themselves

D. **Entrepreneurial Leadership**—leadership that is based on the attitude that the leader is self-employed

Chapter Fifteen - Leadership

V. CURRENT TOPICS IN LEADERSHIP

    A. Substitutes for Leadership

Substitute leadership theory attempts to identify those situations in which the input of leader behavior is partly or wholly canceled out by characteristics of the subordinates or the organization.

    B. Women as Leaders

The **glass ceiling** is the subtle barrier of negative attitudes and prejudices that prevents women from reaching seemingly attainable top-management positions.

    C. Ways Women Lead

Today's women managers often describe their leadership styles as transformational—getting workers to transform or subordinate their individual self-interests into group consensus directed toward a broader goal.

Test Your Knowledge

Essay

1. List and discuss the four forces within a manager that influence their determination of how to make decisions as a leader. (p. 330)

2. List and discuss the two main types of leader behaviors according to the OSU studies. (p. 335)

3. Define the contingency theory of leadership and identify the three primary factors that should be considered when moving leaders into situations appropriate for their leadership styles. (p. 338)

4. List and discuss the four primary types of leader behaviors according to the path-goal theory of leadership. (p. 340)

5. List and discuss three primary behavioral characteristics of a successful coaching leader. (p. 343)

True-False

T F   1. Leadership and management are the same. (p. 327)

T F   2. Leadership is usually goal oriented. (p. 327)

T F   3. The trait theory of leadership is the most cutting edge perspective on leaders. (p. 327)

T F   4. The Tannenbaum-Schmidt continuum goes from boss-centered to subordinate-centered. (p. 329)

T F   5. The VYJ Model focuses in on how much participation to allow subordinates in the decision process. (p. 332)

T F   6. The two main types of behaviors in the OSU studies are structure behavior and (p. 335)
           consideration behavior.

T F   7. Leadership style is a behavioral pattern. (p. 335)

T F   8. Maturity is an aspect of the Hersey-Blanchard life cycle theory of leadership. (p. 336)

T F   9. Fiedler's leadership theory is built on contingencies. (p. 338)

T F   10. Part of the path-goal theory is leadership behavior. (p. 340)

Multiple Choice

1. Leadership is a process of what? (p. 326)
   a. Controlling
   b. Organizing
   c. Directing
   d. Planning

2. Which approach to leadership does the author argue is outdated? (p. 327)
   a. Situational
   b. Behavioral
   c. Contextual
   d. Trait

3. The most effective managers over the long term are also what? (p. 327)
   a. Leaders
   b. Megamanagers
   c. Supermanagers
   d. None are correct

4. The _____ is a relatively modern view of leadership that suggests that (p. 329)
   successful leadership requires a unique combination of leaders, followers, and
   leadership situations.
   a. trait approach to leadership
   b. situational approach to leadership
   c. contingency theory of leadership
   d. task-oriented approach to leadership

5. Subordinate-centered leadership gives a degree of what to the employee? (p. 329)
   a. More supervision
   b. Planning
   c. Freedom
   d. None are correct

6. The VYJ model assumes how many ways or styles for leaders to make decisions? (p. 332)
   a. 1
   b. 3
   c. 5
   d. 7

Chapter Fifteen - Leadership

7. The two main types of behavior in the OSU model were what? (p. 335)
   a. People and task orientation
   b. Structure behavior and consideration behavior
   c. Leadership and followership
   d. None are correct

8. _____ is any leadership activity that delineates the relationship between the leader and the leader's followers or establishes well-defined procedures that followers should adhere to in performing their jobs. (p. 335)
   a. Consideration behavior
   b. Transformational behavior
   c. Structure behavior
   d. Employee-centered behavior

9. Leadership behavior that reflects friendship, mutual trust, respect, and warmth in the relationship between leader and followers is called _____. (p. 335)
   a. structure behavior
   b. consideration behavior
   c. job-centered behavior
   d. psychological behavior

10. _____ is leader behavior that focuses primarily on the work a subordinate is doing. (p. 336)
    a. Consideration behavior
    b. Job-centered behavior
    c. Employee-centered behavior
    d. Transformational behavior

11. Leader behavior that focuses primarily on subordinates as people is called _____. (p. 336)
    a. structure behavior
    b. job-centered behavior
    c. employee-centered behavior
    d. task oriented behavior

12. In the Hersey-Blanchard theory, the maturity of whom is at issue? (p. 336)
    a. Leader
    b. Management
    c. Customers
    d. Followers

13. Leadership _____ is the ability to change leadership styles. (p. 338)
    a. ability
    b. flexibility
    c. knowledge
    d. skill

Chapter Fifteen - Leadership

14. Which of the following is NOT one of the three primary factors that should be considered when moving leaders into situations appropriate for their leadership styles? (p. 338)
    a. leader-member relations
    b. position power
    c. task-structure
    d. company strategy

15. _____ is determined by the extent to which the leader has control over the rewards and punishments followers receive. (p. 339)
    a. Leader-member relations
    b. Task structure
    c. Company strategy
    d. Position power

16. Which of the following leader behaviors is aimed at seeking suggestions from followers regarding business operations to the extent that followers are involved in making important organizational decisions? (p. 340)
    a. Directive behavior
    b. Supportive behavior
    c. Participative behavior
    d. Achievement behavior

17. _____ is aimed at telling followers what to do and how to do it. (p. 340)
    a. Directive behavior
    b. Supportive behavior
    c. Participative behavior
    d. Achievement behavior

18. Leadership that inspires organizational success by profoundly affecting followers' beliefs in what an organization should be, as well as their values, such as justice and integrity is called _____. (p. 342)
    a. transactional leadership
    b. task-oriented leadership
    c. job-centered leadership
    d. transformational leadership

19. Transformation leaders do which of the following? (p. 342)
    a. Inspire
    b. Order
    c. Situate
    d. None are correct

20. _____ is leadership that inspires organizational success by showing followers how to lead themselves. (p. 343)
    a. Transactional leadership
    b. Transformational leadership
    c. Employee-centered leadership
    d. Superleadership

Chapter Fifteen - Leadership

Fill-In

1. Overall, _____ limits the self-guidance of followers in the performance of their tasks, but while it can be relatively firm, it is never rude or malicious. (p. 335)

2. _____ generally aims to develop and maintain a good human relationship between the leader and the followers. (p. 335)

3. The behavioral pattern a leader establishes while guiding organization members in appropriate directions is called _____. (p. 335)

4. The _____ is a leadership concept that hypothesizes that leadership style should reflect primarily the maturity level of the followers. (p. 336)

5. _____ is the degree to which the leader feels accepted by the followers. (p. 339)

6. The degree to which the goals—the work to be done—and other situational factors are outlined clearly is called _____. (p. 339)

7. _____ is aimed at being friendly with followers and showing interest in them as human beings. (p. 340)

8. _____ is aimed at setting challenging goals for followers to reach and expressing and demonstrating confidence that they will measure up to the challenge. (p. 340)

9. A leadership that instructs followers on how to meet the special organizational challenges they face is called _____. (p. 343)

10. _____ is leadership that is based on the attitude that the leader is self-employed. (p. 344)

Answers

Essay

1. The four forces within a manager that influence their determination of how to make decisions as a leader include:
   a. The manager's values, such as the relative importance to the manager of organizational efficiency, personal growth, the growth of subordinates, and company profits
   b. The managers level of confidence in subordinates
   c. The manager's personal leadership strengths
   d. The manager's tolerance for ambiguity

2. The two main types of leader behaviors according to the OSU studies are as follows:
   a. **Structure behavior** – any leadership activity that delineates the relationship between the leader and the leader's followers or establishes well-defined procedures that followers should adhere to in performing their jobs
   b. **Consideration behavior** – leadership behavior that reflects friendship, mutual trust, respect, and warmth in the relationship between leader and follower

3. The **contingency theory of leadership** is a leadership concept that hypothesizes that, in any given leadership situation, leader-member relations, task structure, and the position power of the leader are the three primary factors that should be considered when moving leaders into situations appropriate for their leadership styles.

Chapter Fifteen - Leadership

4. The four primary types of leader behaviors according to the path-goal theory of leadership are:
   a. **Directive behavior** – aimed at telling followers what to do and how to do it. The leader indicates what performance goals exist and precisely what must be done to achieve them.
   b. **Supportive behavior** – aimed at being friendly with follows and showing interest in them as human beings. Through supportive behavior, the leader demonstrates sensitivity to the personal needs of followers.
   c. **Participative behavior** – aimed at seeking suggestions from followers regarding business operations to the extent that followers are involved in making important organizational decisions.
   d. **Achievement behavior** – aimed at setting challenging goals for followers to reach and expressing and demonstrating confidence that they will measure up to the challenge.

5. The three behavior characteristics of a successful coaching leader are:
   a. **Listens closely** – the coaching leader tries to gather both the facts in what is said and the feelings and emotions behind what is said. Such a leader is careful to really listen and not fall into the trap of immediately rebutting statements made by followers.
   b. **Gives emotional support** – the coaching leader gives followers personal encouragement. Such encouragement should constantly be aimed at motivating them to do their best to meet the high demands of successful organizations.
   c. **Shows by example what constitutes appropriate behavior** – the coaching leader shows followers how to handle an employee problem or a production glitch. By demonstrating expertise, the coaching leader builds the trust and respect of followers.

True-False

1. F	3. F	5. T	7. T	9. T
2. T	4. T	6. T	8. T	10. T

Multiple Choice

1. c	5. c	9. b	13. b	17. a
2. d	6. d	10. b	14. d	18. d
3. a	7. b	11. c	15. d	19. a
4. b	8. c	12. d	16. c	20. d

Fill-In

1. structure behavior
2. Consideration behavior
3. leadership style
4. life cycle theory of leadership
5. Leader-member relations
6. task structure
7. Supportive behavior
8. Achievement behavior
9. coaching
10. Entrepreneurial leadership

Modern Management (9th ed.)
Part 5 - Influencing
Chapter Sixteen - Motivation

Overview

This chapter covers the important concept of motivation from defining the process to motivating organizational members. The process theories and content theories of motivation are also discussed. The importance of motivation as well as strategies concerning motivation are also included.

Chapter Outline

Introductory Case: Bristol-Myers Squibb Stresses Motivation in Internet Implementation

I. THE MOTIVATION PROCESS

   A. Defining Motivation

      A. **Motivation** is the inner state that causes an individual to behave in a way that ensures the accomplishment of some goal.
      B. **Process theories of motivation** are explanations of motivation that emphasize how individuals are motivated.
      C. **Content theories of motivation** are explanations of motivation that emphasize people's internal characteristics.

   B. Process Theories of Motivation

      1. There are four important process theories:

         a. **The needs-goal theory** – a motivation model that hypothesizes that felt needs cause human behavior
         b. **The Vroom expectancy theory** – a motivation theory that hypothesizes that felt needs cause human behavior and that motivation strength depends on an individual's degree of desire to perform a behavior
         c. **The equity theory** – an explanation of motivation that emphasizes the individual's perceived fairness of an employment situation and how perceived inequities can cause certain behaviors
         d. **The Porter-Lawler theory** – a motivation theory that hypothesizes that felt needs cause human behavior and that effort expended to accomplish a task is determined by the perceived value of rewards that will result from finishing the task and the probability that those rewards will materialize

            1. **Intrinsic rewards** are rewards that come directly from performing a task.
            2. **Extrinsic rewards** are rewards that are extraneous to the task accomplished.

II. CONTENT THEORIES OF MOTIVATION: HUMAN NEEDS

   A. There are four important content theories:

1. Maslow's hierarchy of needs

   a. **Physiological needs** relate to the normal functioning of the body.
   b. **Security, or safety, needs** relate to the individual's desire to be free from harm, including both bodily and economic disaster.
   c. **Social needs** include the desire for love, companionship, and friendship.
   d. **Esteem needs** are concerned with the desire for respect.
   e. **Self-actualization needs** refer to the desire to maximize whatever potential an individual possesses.

2. Alderfer's ERG theory

   a. **Existence needs** – the need for physical well-being
   b. **Relatedness needs** – the need for satisfying interpersonal relationships
   c. **Growth needs** – the need for continuing personal growth and development

3. Argyris' maturity-immaturity continuum

   a. From a state of passivity as an infant to a state of increasing activity as an adult
   b. From a state of dependence on others as an infant to a state of relative independence as an adult
   c. From being capable of behaving only in a few ways as an infant to being capable of behaving in many ways as an adult
   d. From having erratic, casual, shallow, and quickly dropped interests as an infant to having deeper, more lasting interests as an adult
   e. From having a short time perspective as an infant to having a much longer time perspective as an adult
   f. From being in a subordinate position as an infant to aspiring to occupy and equal or superordinate position as an adult
   g. From a lack of self-awareness as an infant to awareness and control over self as an adult

4. McClelland's acquired needs theory

   a. **Need for achievement** – the desire to do something better or more efficiently than it has even been done before
   b. **Need for power** – the desire to control, influence, or be responsible for others
   c. **Need for affiliation** – the desire to maintain close, friendly personal relationships

III. MOTIVATING ORGANIZATIONAL MEMBERS

   A. The importance of motivating organizational members

   Unsatisfied needs can lead organization members to perform either appropriate or inappropriate behavior.

   B. Strategies for motivating organizational members

   1. **Managerial communication** – perhaps the most basic motivation strategy for managers is to communicate well with organization members

2. Theory X-Theory Y and Theory Z

   a. **Theory X** is a set of essentially negative assumptions about human nature.
   b. **Theory Y** is a set of essentially positive assumptions about human nature.
   c. **Theory Z** is the effectiveness dimension that implies that managers who use either Theory X or Theory Y assumptions when dealing with people can be successful, depending on their situation.

3. Job Design

   a. **Job rotation** – the process of moving workers from one job to another rather than requiring them to perform only one simple and specialized over the long term
   b. **Job enlargement** – the process of increasing the number of operations an individual performs in a job
   c. **Job enrichment** – the process of incorporating motivators into a job situation

      1. **Hygiene, or maintenance, factors** are items that influence the degree of job dissatisfaction.
      2. **Motivating factors, or motivators**, are items that influence the degree of job satisfaction.

   d. **Flextime** – a program that allows workers to complete their jobs within a workweek of a normal number of hours that they schedule themselves

4. **Behavioral modification** – a program that focuses on managing human activity by controlling the consequences of performing that activity

   a. **Positive reinforcement** is a reward that consists of a desirable consequence of behavior.
   b. **Negative reinforcement** is a reward that consists of the elimination of an undesirable consequence of behavior.
   c. **Punishment** is the presentation of an undesirable behavior consequence or the removal of a desirable one that decreases the likelihood that the behavior will continue.

5. Likert's management systems

   a. **System 1** – this style of management is characterized by a lack of confidence or trust in subordinates
   b. **System 2** – this style of management is characterized by a condescending master-to-servant style confidence and trust in subordinates
   c. **System 3** – this style of management is characterized by substantial, though not complete, confidence in subordinates
   d. **System 4** – this style of management is characterized by complete trust and confidence in subordinates

6. Monetary incentives

   Many organizations have found that by putting more of their employees' pay at risk, they can peg more of their total wage costs to sales, which makes expenses more controllable in a downturn.

7. Nonmonetary incentives

   An example of a nonmonetary incentive is one that emphasizes quality, on the theory that most workers are unhappy when they know their work goes to producing a shoddy product.

Test Your Knowledge

Essay

1. List and discuss the five basic needs according to Maslow's hierarchy of needs. (p. 358)
2. Discuss the three basic categories of needs according to Alderfer's ERG theory. (p. 359)
3. List and discuss the three needs human beings develop in their lifetimes according to McClelland's acquired needs theory. (p. 360)
4. Discuss the differences between Theory X and Theory Y managers. (p. 362)
5. List and discuss the four systems, according to Likert, in which management styles can be categorized. (p. 368)

True-False

T F 1. Motivation is primarily an outer state caused by the manager's supervision. (p. 354)

T F 2. One process theory of motivation is Maslow's hierarchy of needs. (p. 354)

T F 3. Content theories deal with people's internal characteristics. (p. 354)

T F 4. The expectancy theory is based on the degree of the person's desire to perform a behavior. (p. 355)

T F 5. Equity theory is based on a fairness in the workplace criterion. (p. 356)

T F 6. Intrinsic rewards are rewards that are extraneous to the task accomplished. (p. 357)

T F 7. The last step in Maslow's hierarchy is esteem needs. (p. 358)

T F 8. Under McClelland's acquired needs theory, power and affiliation are much more important than achievement. (p. 360)

T F 9. Theory X holds basically good assumptions about human behavior. (p. 362)

T F 10. Job rotation always enriches a job. (p. 363)

Chapter Sixteen - Motivation

Multiple Choice

1. Motivation is an _____ state. (p. 354)
   a. external
   b. internal
   c. outside
   d. None are correct

2. _____ of motivation are explanations of motivation that emphasize how individuals are motivated. (p. 354)
   a. Process theories
   b. Content theories
   c. Maslow's theories
   d. Achievement theories

3. Which of the following theories of motivation are explanations of motivation that emphasize people's internal characteristics? (p. 354)
   a. Process theories of motivation
   b. Content theories of motivation
   c. Maslow's theories of motivation
   d. Achievement theories of motivation

4. The needs-goal theory posits _____. (p. 354)
   a. felt needs cause human behavior
   b. managers create behavior
   c. beliefs cause human behavior
   d. None are correct

5. Key aspects of the Porter-Lawler motivational theory are _____ (p. 356)
   a. needs and goals
   b. a hierarchy of needs
   c. intrinsic and extrinsic rewards
   d. an equity of needs

6. Maslow's _____ relate to the individual's desire to be free from harm, including both bodily and economic disaster. (p. 358)
   a. physiological needs
   b. safety needs
   c. social needs
   d. esteem needs

7. Maslow's _____ are concerned with the desire for respect. (p. 358)
   a. physiological needs
   b. safety needs
   c. social needs
   d. esteem needs

8. Under Maslow's hierarchy of needs, if an individual's potential is fulfilled it is referred (p. 359) to as _____.
   a. meeting esteem needs
   b. meeting social needs
   c. becoming affiliated
   d. becoming self-actualized

9. _____ is an explanation of human needs that divides them into three basic (p. 359) types: existence needs, relatedness needs, and growth needs.
   a. Alderfer's ERG theory
   b. McClelland's acquired needs theory
   c. Achievement theory
   d. Maslow's theory

10. The ERG theory is very similar to what other theorist's approach to motivation? (p. 360)
    a. Likert
    b. Maslow
    c. Taylor
    d. McClelland

11. Which of the following is a strategy for motivating organizational members? (p. 362)
    a. Managerial communication
    b. Job design
    c. Behavior modification
    d. All are correct

12. _____ is a set of essentially negative assumptions about human nature. (p. 363)
    a. Theory X
    b. Theory Y
    c. Theory Z
    d. Theory S

13. Which of the following is a set of essentially positive assumptions about human nature? (p. 363)
    a. Theory X
    b. Theory Y
    c. Theory Z
    d. Theory S

14. _____ is the process of moving workers from one job to another rather than (p. 363) requiring them to perform only one simple and specialized job over the long run.
    a. Job rotation
    b. Job enrichment
    c. Job enlargement
    d. Job specialization

Chapter Sixteen - Motivation

15. The process of increasing the number of operations an individual performs in a job is called _____. (p. 364)
    a. job rotation
    b. job enrichment
    c. job enlargement
    d. job specialization

16. _____ is the process of incorporating motivators into a job situation. (p. 364)
    a. Job rotation
    b. Job enrichment
    c. Job enlargement
    d. Job specialization

17. Under Herzberg's theory what factors influence the degree of job dissatisfaction? (p. 364)
    a. Motivational
    b. Managerial
    c. Hygiene
    d. None are correct

18. What did Eli Lilly use to create organizational benefits? (p. 364)
    a. Job overhaul
    b. Job rotation
    c. Job enrichment
    d. None were used

19. _____ is a program that allows workers to complete their jobs within a workweek of a normal number of hours that they schedule themselves. (p. 365)
    a. Coretime
    b. Flextime
    c. Cafeteriatime
    d. Benefitstime

20. A reward that consists of a desirable consequence of behavior is called _____. (p. 367)
    a. positive reinforcement
    b. negative reinforcement
    c. punishment
    d. obsolescence

Fill-In

1. _____ is an individual's degree of desire to perform a behavior. (p. 355)

2. Rewards that come directly from performing a task are called _____. (p. 357)

3. _____ are rewards that are extraneous to the task accomplished. (p. 357)

4. Maslow's _____ relate to the normal functioning of the body. (p. 358)

5. Maslow's _____ include the desire for love, companionship, and friendship. (p. 358)

6. The desire to do something better or more efficiently than it has even been done before is referred to as _____. (p. 360)

7. _____ is the desire to maintain close, friendly personal relationships. (p. 360)

8. _____ are items that influence the degree of job satisfaction. (p. 364)

9. A program that allows workers to complete their jobs within a workweek of a normal number of hours that they schedule themselves is called _____. (p. 365)

10. _____ is a program that focuses on managing human activity by controlling the consequences of performing that activity. (p. 366)

Answers

Essay

1. The five basic needs according to Maslow's Hierarchy of Needs are as follows:
    a. **Physiological needs** – needs for the normal functioning of the body, including the desires for water, food, rest, and air
    b. **Security, or safety, needs** – reflects the human desire to keep free from physical harm
    c. **Social needs** – reflects the human desire to belong, including longings for friendship, companionship, and love
    d. **Esteem needs** – includes the desire for self-respect and respect from others
    e. **Self-actualization needs** – reflects the human desire to maximize personal potential

2. The three basic categories of needs according to Alderfer's ERG theory include:
    a. **Existence needs** – the need for physical well-being
    b. **Relatedness needs** – the need for satisfying interpersonal relationships
    c. **Growth needs** – the need for continuing personal growth and development

3. The three needs according to McClelland's acquired needs theory are as follows:
    a. **Need for achievement** – the desire to do something better or more efficiently than it has even been before
    b. **Need for power** – the desire to control, influence, or be responsible for others
    c. **Need for affiliation** – the desire to maintain close, friendly personal relationships

4. **Theory X** involves negative assumptions about people that managers often use as the basis for dealing with their subordinates. It is a set of essentially negative assumptions about human nature. **Theory Y** represents positive assumptions about people that manager should strive to use. It is essentially as set of positive assumptions about human nature.

5. The four systems, according to Likert, in which management styles can be categorized include:
    a. **System 1** – this style of management is characterized by a lack of confidence or trust in subordinates
    b. **System 2** – this style of management is characterized by a condescending master-to-servant style confidence and trust in subordinates
    c. **System 3** – this style of management is characterized by substantial, though not complete, confidence in subordinates
    d. **System 4** – this style of management is characterized by complete trust and confidence in subordinates

Chapter Sixteen - Motivation

True-False

1. F
2. F
3. T
4. T
5. T
6. F
7. F
8. F
9. F
10. F

Multiple Choice

1. b
2. a
3. b
4. a
5. c
6. b
7. d
8. d
9. a
10. b
11. d
12. a
13. b
14. a
15. c
16. b
17. c
18. b
19. b
20. a

Fill-In

1. Motivation strength
2. intrinsic rewards
3. Extrinsic rewards
4. physiological needs
5. social needs
6. need for achievement
7. need for affiliation
8. Motivators
9. flextime
10. Behavior modification

Modern Management (9th ed.)
Part 5 - Influencing
Chapter Seventeen – Groups, Teams, and Corporate Culture

Overview

This chapter takes you through the concepts of groups, teams, and corporate culture. It explains the difference between formal and informal groups, explores the types of formal groups in organizations, and describes the roles of managers within groups. An appreciation of teams and how they can be managed is also presented.

Chapter Outline

Introductory Case: Teamwork Builds Success at Xerox

I. GROUPS

   A **group** is any number of people who (1) interact with one another; (2) are psychologically aware of one another, and (3) perceive themselves to be a group.

II. KINDS OF GROUPS IN ORGANIZATIONS

   A. Formal groups

      1. A **formal group** is a group that exists in an organization by virtue of management decree to perform tasks that enhance the attainment of organizational objectives.

         a. **Command groups** are formal groups that are outlined in the chain of command on an organization chart.
         b. **Task groups** are formal groups of organization members who interact with one another to accomplish most of the organization's nonroutine tasks.
         c. A **committee** is a group of individuals charged with performing some type of specific activity and is usually classified as a task group.
         d. Four major reasons to establish a committee:
            1. To allow organization members to exchange ideas
            2. To generate suggestions and recommendations that can be offered to other organizational units
            3. To develop new ideas for solving existing organizational problems
            4. To assist in the development of organizational policies
         e. **Groupthink** is the mode of thinking that group members engage in when the desire for agreement so dominates the group that it overrides the need to realistically appraise alternative problem solutions.
         f. **Work teams** are task groups used in organizations to achieve greater organizational flexibility or to cope with rapid growth.

      2. Stages of formal group development

         a. The acceptance stage
         b. The communication and decision-making stage
         c. The group solidarity stage
         d. The group control

B. Informal groups

  1. An **informal group** is a collection of individuals whose common work experiences result in the development of a system of interpersonal relations that extend beyond those established by management.

  2. Kinds of informal groups

     a. An **interest group** is an informal group that gains and maintains membership primarily because of a common concern members have about a specific issue.
     b. A **friendship group** is an informal group that forms in organizations because of the personal affiliation members have with one another.

  3. Benefits of informal group membership

III. MANAGING WORK GROUPS

  A. Determining Group Existence

   1. **Sociometry** is an analytical tool that can be used to determine what informal groups exist in an organization and who the members of those groups are.

   2. A **sociogram** is a sociometric diagram that summarizes the personal feelings of organization members about the people in the organization with whom they would like to spend free time.

  B. Understanding the Evolution of informal groups

   1. Homan's Model – perhaps the most widely accepted framework for explaining the evolution of informal groups

IV. TEAMS

  A. Groups versus Teams

  A **team** is a group whose members influence one another toward the accomplishment of (an) organizational objective(s).

  B. Types of Teams in Organizations

   1. A **problem-solving team** is an organizational team set up to help eliminate a specified problem within the organization.

   2. A **self-managed team** is an organizational team established to plan, organize, influence, and control its own work situation with only minimal direction from management.

   3. A **cross-functional team** is an organizational team composed of people from different functional areas of the organization who are all focused on a specified objective.

C. Stages of Team Development

1. Forming – during this stage, members of the newly formed team become oriented to the team and acquainted with one another
2. Storming – characterized by conflict and disagreement as team members become more assertive in clarifying their individual roles
3. Norming – characterized by agreement among team members on roles, rules, and acceptable behavior while working on the team
4. Performing – at this stage, the team fully focuses on solving organizational problems and on meeting assigned challenges
5. Adjourning – this stage normally occurs only in teams established for some special purpose to be accomplished in a limited time period

D. Team Effectiveness

1. People-related factors
2. Organization-related factors
3. Task-related factors
4. Effective team performance

E. Trust and Effective Teams
1. Strategies used to build trust in groups include:
    a. Communicate often to team members
    b. Show respect for team members
    c. Be fair to team members
    d. Be predictable
    e. Demonstrate competence

V. CORPORATE CULTURE

A. **Corporate culture** is defined as a set of shared values and beliefs that organizational members have regarding the functioning and existence of their organization.

B. Factors can include status symbols, traditions and history, and the physical environment.

C. The Significance of Corporate Culture

1. The corporate culture impacts the behavior of everyone in the organization and focuses attention to certain interests and areas.

Test Your Knowledge

Essay

1. List and discuss the four major reasons that managers would establish committees. (p. 378)

2. List and discuss five traits that characterize members of a group that reaches maximum maturity and effectiveness. (p. 381)

Chapter Seventeen – Groups, Teams, and Corporate Culture

3. Discuss the four group member benefits that result in the development of informal groups in organizations. (p. 383)

4. List and discuss the three types of teams commonly found in today's organizations. (p. 387)

5. Discuss the five primary mechanisms that are necessary for the development and reinforcement of a desired corporate culture. (p. 392)

True-False

T F   1. Formal groups exist because of management decree. (p. 376)

T F   2. A task group usually is brought together to perform a routine task. (p. 377)

T F   3. A command group is a type of team. (p. 377)

T F   4. An example of a formal group is a committee. (p. 378)

T F   5. Procedural steps can make a committee successful. (p. 379)

T F   6. A work team is a task group (p. 379)

T F   7. The first stage of formal group development is the communication and decision-making stage. (p. 381)

T F   8. An informal group is based on interpersonal relationships. (p. 382)

T F   9. A sociometric analysis can be used to determine the existence of a group. (p. 383)

T F   10. Groups and teams are the same things. (p. 386)

Multiple Choice

1. A formal group exists because of management _____. (p. 376)
    a. Hopes
    b. Decree
    c. Wishes
    d. Knowledge

2. A _____ is a formal group that is outlined on the organization chart in its hierarchy. (p. 377)
    a. task group
    b. cross-functional group
    c. command group
    d. friendship group

3. A(n) _____ is a formal group of organization members who interact with one another to accomplish nonroutine organizational tasks. (p. 377)
    a. task group
    b. cross-functional group
    c. interest group
    d. committee

Chapter Seventeen – Groups, Teams, and Corporate Culture

4. A(n) _____ is a task group that is charged with performing some type of specific activity. (p. 378)
   a. virtual group
   b. cross-functional group
   c. friendship group
   d. committee

5. _____ is the mode of thinking where there is great pressure to ensure agreement. (p. 379)
   a. Conformity pressures
   b. Group behavior
   c. Team management
   d. Groupthink

6. A work team is a _____. (p. 379)
   a. task group
   b. cross-functional team
   c. hierarchical group
   d. None are correct

7. What type of group is an interest group? (p. 382)
   a. Formal
   b. Informal
   c. Management
   d. Worker

8. A(n) _____ is an informal group that forms in organizations because of the personal affiliation that members have with one another. (p. 382)
   a. command group
   b. task group
   c. friendship group
   d. committee

9. What tool can be used to determine which informal groups exist? (p. 383)
   a. Statistics
   b. Observation
   c. Sociometry
   d. None are correct

10. A(n) _____ is a sociometric diagram that summarizes the personal feelings of organization members about the people in the organization with whom they would like to spend free time. (p. 383)
    a. sociogram
    b. histogram
    c. perceptual map
    d. pie chart

Chapter Seventeen – Groups, Teams, and Corporate Culture

11. A _____ team is an organized team set up to help eliminate a specified problem within the organization. (p. 386)
    a. management
    b. worker
    c. board
    d. problem-solving

12. What type of team structure did Harley-Davidson use? (p. 387)
    a. Problem-solving
    b. Creative taskforce
    c. Customer-work team
    d. Cross-functional team

13. A(n) _____ is an organizational team established to plan, organize, influence, and control its own work situation with only minimal direction from management. (p. 387)
    a. problem-solving team
    b. cross-functional team
    c. interest team
    d. self-managed team

14. An organizational team composed of people from different functional areas of the organization who are all focused on a specified objective is called a(n) _____. (p. 387)
    a. problem-solving team
    b. cross-functional team
    c. interest team
    d. self-managed team

15. During the _____ stage of team development, members of the newly formed team become oriented to the team and acquainted with one another. (p. 388)
    a. forming
    b. storming
    c. norming
    d. performing

16. The _____ stage of team development is characterized by conflict and disagreement as team members become more assertive in clarifying their individual roles. (p. 389)
    a. forming
    b. storming
    c. norming
    d. performing

17. The _____ stage of team development is characterized by agreement among team members on roles, rules, and acceptable behavior while working on the team. (p. 389)
    a. forming
    b. storming
    c. norming
    d. performing

Chapter Seventeen – Groups, Teams, and Corporate Culture

18. The fourth stage of the team development process is _____. (p. 389)
    a. forming
    b. storming
    c. norming
    d. performing

19. _____ is the stage of the team development process in which the team finishes its job and prepares to disband. (p. 389)
    a. storming
    b. norming
    c. performing
    d. adjourning

20. What is a set of shared values and beliefs? (p. 391)
    a. Corporate culture
    b. Management decrees
    c. Board directives
    d. None are correct

Fill-In

1. _____ typically handle routine organizational activities. (p. 377)

2. A(n) _____ is defined as a collection of individuals whose common work experiences result in the development of a system of interpersonal relations that extend beyond those established by management. (p. 382)

3. An example of a(n) _____ is a group of workers pressing management for better pay or working conditions. (p. 382)

4. _____ is an analytical tool that can be used to determine what informal groups exist in an organization and who the members of those groups are. (p. 383)

5. The typical _____ has 5 to 12 members and is formed to discuss ways to improve quality in all phases of the organization or to improve the overall work environment. (p. 386)

6. _____ is the first stage of the team development process. (p. 388)

7. Conflicts generated during the storming stage of team development are resolved in the _____. (p. 389)

8. During the _____ of team development, managers should recognize the team's accomplishments regularly, for productive team behavior must be reinforced to enhance the probability that it will continue in the future. (p. 389)

9. Managers should recognize team members' disappointment and sense of loss as normal during the _____ of team development. (p. 389)

10. _____ is a set of shared values and beliefs that organization members have regarding the functioning and existence of their organization. (p. 391)

Chapter Seventeen – Groups, Teams, and Corporate Culture

Answers

Essay

1. <u>The four major reasons that managers would establish committees include:</u>
   a. To allow organization members to exchange ideas
   b. To generate suggestions and recommendations that can be offered to other organizational units
   c. To develop new ideas for solving existing organizational problems
   d. To assist in the development of organizational policies

2. <u>The five traits that characterize members of a group that reach maximum maturity and effectiveness include:</u>
   a. **Members function as a unit** – the group works as a team. Members do not disturb one another to the point of interfering with their collaboration.
   b. **Members participate effectively in group effort** – members work hard when there is something to do. They seldom loaf, even if they have the opportunity to do so.
   c. **Members are oriented toward a single goal** – group members work for the common purpose; they do not waste group resources by moving in different directions.
   d. **Members have the equipment, tools, and skills necessary to attain the group's goals** – members are taught the various parts of their jobs by experts and strive to acquire whatever resources they need to attain group objectives.
   e. **Members ask and receive suggestions, opinions, and information from one another** – a member who is uncertain about something stops working and asks another member for information. Group members generally talk to one another openly and frequently.

3. <u>The four group member benefits that result in the development of informal groups in organizations are:</u>
   a. Perpetuation of social and cultural values that group members consider important
   b. Status and social satisfaction that people might not enjoy without group membership
   c. Increased ease of communication among group members
   d. Increased desirability of the overall work environment

4. <u>The three types of teams commonly found in today's organizations include:</u>
   a. **Problem-solving team** – an organizational team set up to help eliminate a specified problem within the organization
   b. **Self-managed team** – an organizational team established to plan, organize, influence, and control its own work situation with only minimal direction from management
   c. **Cross-functional team** – an organizational team composed of people from different functional areas of the organization who are all focused on a specified objective

5. <u>The five primary mechanisms that are necessary for the development and reinforcement of a desired corporate culture include:</u>
   a. **What leaders pay attention to, measure, and control** – leaders can communicate very effectively what their vision of the organization is and what they want done by consistently emphasizing the same issues in meetings, in casual remarks and questions, and in strategy discussions
   b. **Leaders' reactions to critical incidents and organizational crises** – the manner in which leaders deal with crises can create new beliefs and values and reveal underlying organizational assumptions
   c. **Deliberate role modeling, teaching, and coaching** – the behaviors of leaders in both formal and informal settings have an important effect on employee beliefs, values, and behaviors

Chapter Seventeen – Groups, Teams, and Corporate Culture

d. **Criteria for allocation of reward and status** – leaders can firmly communicate their priorities and values by consistently linking rewards and punishments to the behaviors that concern them
e. **Criteria for recruitment, selection, promotion, and retirement of employee** – the kinds of people who are hired and who succeed in an organization are those who accept the organization's values and behave accordingly

True-False

1. T
2. F
3. F
4. T
5. T
6. T
7. F
8. F
9. T
10. F

Multiple Choice

1. b
2. c
3. a
4. d
5. d
6. a
7. b
8. c
9. c
10. a
11. d
12. d
13. d
14. b
15. a
16. b
17. c
18. d
19. d
20. d

Fill-In

1. Command groups
2. informal group
3. interest group
4. Sociometry
5. problem-solving team
6. Forming
7. norming stage
8. performing stage
9. adjourning stage
10. Corporate culture

Modern Management (9th ed.)
Part 5 - Influencing
Chapter Eighteen – Understanding People: Attitudes, Perception, and Learning

Overview

This chapter explores the task of understanding employee workplace attitudes as well as insights into how to alter employee attitudes. In addition, it explains and guides us to appreciate the impact of employee perceptions on employee behavior. Also included are the concepts of procedural justice and understanding adult learners.

Chapter Outline

Introductory Case: Where was the People Focus at Webvan?

I. WHAT ARE ATTITUDES?

   A. An **attitude** is a predisposition to react to a situation, person, or concepts with a particular response.

      1. There are three major components:

         a. **Cognitive** – information and beliefs about a particular person or object
         b. **Affective** – a positive or negative feeling about a particular person or object
         c. **Behavioral** – an intent or desire to behave in a certain way toward a particular person or object

   B. How Beliefs and Values Create Attitudes

      1. **Beliefs** are accepted facts or truths about an object or person that have been gained from either direct experience or a secondary source.
      2. **Values** are the global beliefs that guide one's actions and judgments across a variety of situations.

   C. Attitude surveys

   Managers can use **attitude surveys** to predict employee behavior or determine the sources of existing problems.

   D. Theory of Reasoned Action

      1. States that when a behavior is a matter of choice, the best predictor of the behavior is the person's intention to perform.

      2. Employee attitudes

         a. Attitude theory and reasoned action

      3. Changing attitudes

         a. Behaviors and attitudes can best be predicted by knowing two factors:

            1. A person's beliefs

2. The social norms that influence a person's intentions

b. Four major causes of behavioral problems according to human resource specialists

1. Lack of skills
2. Lack of positive attitude
3. Rule breaking
4. Personal problems

II. PERCEPTION

A. Perception and the Perceptual Process

1. **Perception** is the psychological process of selecting stimuli, organizing data into recognizable patterns, and interpreting the resulting information.

2. The **perceptual process** is the series of actions that individuals follow in order to select, organize and interpret stimuli from the environment.

B. Attribution Theory: Interpreting the Behaviors of Others

1. **Attribution** is the process by which people interpret the behavior of others by assigning them motives or causes.

2. Managers can avoid inappropriate attributions in three ways:

a. By making a greater effort to see situations as they are perceived by others
b. By guarding against perceptual distortions
c. By paying more attention to individual differences among subordinates

3. Three factors people generally focus on when making attributions:

a. Consensus
b. Consistency
c. Distinctiveness

C. Perceptual Distortions

1. **Stereotypes** – a fixed, distorted generalization about members of a group
2. **Halo effect** – results from allowing one particular aspect of someone's behavior to influence one's evaluation of all other aspects of that person's behavior
3. **Projection** – the unconscious tendency to assign one's own traits, motives, beliefs, and attitudes to others
4. **Attribution error** – the tendency to overestimate internal causes of behavior and underestimate external ones when judging other people's behavior
5. **Self-serving bias** – the tendency to overestimate external causes of behavior and underestimate internal ones when judging one's own behavior.
6. **Selective perception** – the tendency to collect information that not only supports one's own motives, beliefs and attitudes, but also minimizes the emotional distress caused by unfamiliar or troublesome stimuli

Chapter Eighteen – Understanding People: Attitudes, Perception, and Learning

   D. Perceptions of Procedural Justice

      1. **Procedural justice** is the perceived fairness of the process used for deciding workplace outcomes such as merit increases and promotions.
      2. Procedures and outcomes
      3. Dispute resolution
      4. Employee responses
      5. Measuring employee attitudes

III. LEARNING

   A. **Learning** is a more or less permanent change in behavior resulting from practice, experience, education, or training.

      1. **Operant learning** – an approach that holds the behavior leading to positive consequences is more likely to be repeated
      2. **Cognitive learning** – an approach theory that focuses on thought processes and assumes that human beings have a high capacity to act in a purposeful manner, and so to choose behaviors that will enable them to achieve long-run goals
      3. Goal-setting strategies
      4. Goal setting and problem solving

   B. Learning Strategies

      1. Reinforcement Strategy

         a. **Positive reinforcement** – any stimulus that causes a behavior to be repeated is a positive reinforcer
         b. **Avoidance strategy** – behavior that can prevent the onset of an undesired consequence often results form avoidance learning
         c. **Escape strategy** – when a manager provides an arrangement in which a desired response will terminate an undesired response, that manager is using the escape strategy
         d. **Punishment strategy** – when an undesired behavior by an employee is followed by an undesired response by management, a punishment strategy is being used

Test Your Knowledge

Essay

1. List and discuss the three primary components of attitudes. (p. 400)
2. Discuss the three factors that people generally focus on when making attributions. (p. 407)
3. Explain the halo effect and describe how the halo problem can be minimized. (p. 408)
4. List and discuss four advantages that result from the use of goal setting in organizations. (p. 412)

Chapter Eighteen – Understanding People: Attitudes, Perception, and Learning

5. Discuss the four reinforcement strategies that managers can use to shape or strengthen employee behavior. (p. 413)

True-False

T F 1. Attitude is a predisposition to react. (p. 400)

T F 2. An affective attitude deals with the intent to behave in a certain way. (p. 400)

T F 3. Beliefs are seen as truths. (p. 401)

T F 4. Peer beliefs lead to subjective norms. (p. 403)

T F 5. The human resources approach in this chapter deals with performance appraisal. (p. 404)

T F 6. Nucor Steel uses employee teams to achieve quality. (p. 405)

T F 7. Perception is a kinetic process. (p. 406)

T F 8. In attribution theory, interpretation of behavior is key. (p. 407)

T F 9. A stereotype is a flexible generalization. (p. 408)

T F 10. Procedural justice is perceived fairness. (p. 409)

Multiple Choice

1. What is described as a predisposition to react to a situation, person, or concept? (p. 400)
   a. Values
   b. Beliefs
   c. Attitudes
   d. Stereotype

2. Attitudes have three primary components. Which of the following is NOT one of these components? (p. 400)
   a. Physical
   b. Cognitive
   c. Affective
   d. Behavioral

3. Accepted facts or truths about an object or person that have been gained from either direct experience or a secondary source are called _____. (p. 401)
   a. beliefs
   b. values
   c. attitudes
   d. perceptions

4. Beliefs are considered _____. (p. 401)
   a. accepted facts
   b. accepted values
   c. accepted myths
   d. None is correct

Chapter Eighteen – Understanding People: Attitudes, Perception, and Learning

5. Values are _____ beliefs. (p. 401)
   a. individual
   b. community
   c. national
   d. global

6. Global beliefs that guide one's actions and judgments across a variety of situations are called _____. (p. 401)
   a. beliefs
   b. attitudes
   c. perceptions
   d. values

7. When people are surveyed, they express attitudes on which they are likely to base _____. (p. 402)
   a. thinking
   b. behavior
   c. values
   d. None are correct

8. Intention leads to _____. (p. 403)
   a. attitudes
   b. values
   c. behavior
   d. thinking

9. There are three theories of employee attitudes. Which of the following is NOT one? (p. 403)
   a. Design of structure
   b. Design of job
   c. Social influence
   d. Dispositional approach

10. Perception is a _____ process. (p. 406)
    a. social
    b. mental
    c. physical
    d. psychological

11. The _____ is the series of actions that individuals follow in order to select, organize, and interpret stimuli from the environment. (p. 406)
    a. decision process
    b. perceptual process
    c. value process
    d. belief process

12. Attribution is a process by which people _____ the behavior of others. (p. 407)
    a. think
    b. interpret
    c. know
    d. None are correct

Chapter Eighteen – Understanding People: Attitudes, Perception, and Learning

13. A(n) _____ is a fixed, distorted generalization about members of a group. (p. 408)
    a. attribution
    b. halo effect
    c. projection
    d. stereotype

14. The _____ results from allowing one particular aspect of someone's behavior (p. 408) to influence one's evaluation of all other aspects of that person's behavior.
    a. attribution effect
    b. halo effect
    c. stereotype effect
    d. projection effect

15. _____ is the tendency to overestimate internal causes of behavior and (p. 409) underestimate external ones when judging other people's behaviors.
    a. Attribution error
    b. Self-serving bias
    c. Selective perception
    d. Halo effect

16. The tendency to overestimate the external causes of behavior and underestimate (p. 409) internal ones when judging one's own behavior is called _____.
    a. attribution error
    b. self-serving bias
    c. selective perception
    d. the halo effect

17. _____ is the tendency to collect information that not only supports one's (p. 409) own motives, beliefs and attitudes but also minimizes the emotional distress caused by unfamiliar or troublesome stimuli.
    a. Attribution error
    b. Self-serving bias
    c. Selective perception
    d. Halo effect

18. Projection is the _____ tendency to assign one's own traits, motives, beliefs and (p. 408) attitudes to others.
    a. conscious
    b. premeditated
    c. unconscious
    d. thought out

19. _____ is an approach that holds the behavior leading to positive consequences (p. 411) is more likely to be repeated.
    a. Operant learning
    b. Cognitive learning
    c. Virtual learning
    d. Perceptual learning

Chapter Eighteen – Understanding People: Attitudes, Perception, and Learning

20. An approach theory that focuses on thought processes and assumes that human beings have a high capacity to act in a purposeful manner and so to choose behaviors that will enable them to achieve long-run goals is called _____. (p. 412)
    a. operant learning
    b. cognitive learning
    c. classical learning
    d. perceptual learning

Fill-In

1. _____ tend to be broad views of life and are influenced by parents, peer groups, and associates. (p. 401)

2. The perceived fairness of the process used for deciding workplace outcomes, such as merit increases and promotions, is called _____. (p. 409)

3. _____ is the tendency to overestimate internal causes of behavior and underestimate external ones when judging other people's behavior. (p. 409)

4. _____ is a more or less permanent change in behavior resulting from practice, experience, education, or training. (p. 411)

5. _____ is the theory that assumes human beings have a high capacity to act in a purposeful manner, and so to choose behaviors that will enable them to achieve long-run goals. (p. 412)

6. Managers often use the principle of _____ when attempting to shape employee behavior. (p. 413)

7. Common examples of _____ are praise, recognition, pay and support. (p. 413)

8. Behavior that can prevent the onset of an undesired consequence of results from _____. (p. 413)

9. When a manager provides an arrangement in which a desired response will terminate an undesired consequence, that manager is using the _____. (p. 413)

10. When an undesired behavior by an employee is followed by an undesired response by management, a(n) _____ strategy is being used. (p. 413)

Answers

Essay

1. The three primary components of attitudes include:
    a. **Cognitive** – information and beliefs about a particular person or object
    b. **Affective** – a positive or negative feeling about a particular person or object
    c. **Behavioral** – an intent or desire to behave in a certain way toward a particular person or object

2. The three factors that people generally focus on when making attributions are:
    a. **Consensus** – the extent to which they believe that the person being observed is behaving in a manner consistent with the behavior of his or her peers. High consensus exists when the person's actions reflect, or are similar to, the actions of the groups; low consensus exists when the person's actions do not.

b. **Consistency** – the extent to which they believe that the person being observed behaves consistently—in a similar fashion—when confronted on other occasions with the same or similar situations. High consistency exists when the person repeatedly acts in the same way when faced with similar stimuli.

c. **Distinctiveness** – the extent to which they believe that the person being observed would behave consistently when faced with different situations. Low distinctiveness exists when the person acts in a similar manner in response to different stimuli. High distinctiveness exists when the person varies his or her response in different situations.

3. The **halo effect** results from allowing one particular aspect of someone's behavior to influence one's evaluation of all other aspects of that person's behavior. For example, the manager who knows that a particular employee always arrives at work early and helps to open the business may let the "halo" of the employee's dependability influence his or her perceptions of the employee in other areas. The halo problem can be minimized by supervisory training that focuses on the fact that it is not unusual for employees to perform well in some areas and less effectively in others.

4. The four advantages that result from the use of goal setting in organizations are:
   a. **Directed behavior** – goals help people focus their daily decisions in specific ways
   b. **Challenges** – individuals are more motivated, and achieve higher levels of performance, when given specific objectives instead of such nondirective responses as "keep up the good work"
   c. **Resource allocation** – critical decisions involving resources are more consistent with organizational goals when goal-setting strategies are used
   d. **Structure** – the formal and informal organizational structure can be shaped to set communication patterns and provide each position with a degree of authority and responsibility that supports employee and organizational goals

5. The four reinforcement strategies that managers can use include:
   a. **Positive reinforcement** – any stimulus that causes a behavior to be repeated is a positive reinforcer. Common examples of positive reinforcement are praise, recognition, and pay.
   b. **Avoidance strategy** – behavior that can prevent the onset of an undesired consequence often results from avoidance learning. In recent years, for example, many employers have adopted strict policies regarding the use of illegal drugs by employees.
   c. **Escape strategy** – when a manager provides an arrangement in which a desired response will terminate an undesired consequence, that manager is using the escape strategy. For example, a manager may first set employees the least desired task, such as cleaning and setting up equipment, and inform them that once the equipment has passed inspection, they can move on to a more desirable task.
   d. **Punishment strategy** – when an undesired behavior by an employee is followed by an undesired response by management, a punishment strategy is being used. Organizations commonly select such punishment strategies as oral and written warnings, demotion, suspension, and termination.

True-False

1. T	3. T	5. F	7. F	9. F
2. F	4. T	6. T	8. T	10. T

Multiple Choice

1. c	3. a	5. d	7. b	9. a
2. a	4. a	6. d	8. c	10. d

11. b	13. d	15. a	17. c	19. a
12. b	14. b	16. b	18. c	20. b

Fill-In

1. Values
2. procedural justice
3. Attribution error
4. Learning
5. Cognitive learning
6. reinforcement
7. positive reinforcement
8. avoidance learning
9. escape strategy
10. punishment

Modern Management (9th ed.)
Part 6 - Controlling
Chapter Nineteen – Principles of Controlling

Overview

In this chapter, the management function of control will be discussed. There is a definition of control, an understanding of the subsystems involved, and an appreciation for the types of control. There will also be insights into the concept of power, and its interaction with control and knowledge concerning the barriers to overcome and implement control.

Chapter Outline

Introductory Case: DaimlerChrysler Controls by Initiating Web-Based FastCar

I. THE FUNDAMENTALS OF CONTROLLING

    A. Defining Control

    Control is making something happen the way it was planned to happen.

    B. Defining Controlling

    Controlling is the process managers go through to control.

      1. The controlling subsystems

      2. The controlling process

        a. Measuring performance

          1. How to measure
          2. What to measure

        b. Comparing measured performance to standards

          1. A **standard** is the level of activity established to serve as a model for evaluating organizational performance.

        c. Taking corrective action

          1. **Corrective action** is managerial activity aimed at bringing organizational performance up to the level of performance standards.
          2. **Problems** are factors within an organization that are barriers to organizational goal attainment.
          3. A **symptom** is a sign that a problem exists.

    C. Types of Control

      1. **Precontrol** – control that takes place before some unit of work is actually performed
      2. **Concurrent** – control that takes place as some unit of work is being performed
      3. **Feedback** – control that takes place after some unit of work has been performed

Chapter Nineteen – Principles of Controlling

II. THE CONTROLLER AND CONTROL

    A. The Job of the Controller

        1. The **controller** is a staff person whose basic responsibility is to assist line managers with the controlling function.

        2. The controller usually works with information about the following financial dimensions of the organization:
           a. Profits
           b. Revenues
           c. Costs
           d. Investments
           e. Discretionary expenses

    B. How much control is needed?

    Cost-benefit analysis – the process of comparing the costs of some activity with the benefit or revenue that results from activity to determine the activity's total worth to the organization

III. POWER AND CONTROL

    A. A Definition of Power

    Power is the extent to which an individual is able to influence others so they respond to orders.

    B. Total power of a manager

        1. **Total power** is the entire amount of power an individual in an organization possesses.

           a. **Position power** is power derived from the organizational position a manager holds.
           b. **Personal power** is the power derived from a manager's relationships with others.

    C. Steps for Increasing Total Power

        1. Develop the following attitudes and beliefs in other organization members in order to increase personal power

           a. A sense of obligation toward the manager
           b. A belief that the manager possesses a high level of expertise within the organization
           c. A sense of identification with the manager
           d. The perception that they are dependent on the manager

IV. PERFORMING THE CONTROL FUNCTION

    A. Potential Barriers to Successful Controlling

        1. Long-term versus short-term production
        2. Employee frustration and morale
        3. Filling of reports
        4. Perspective of organizational members
        5. Means versus ends

B. Making Controlling Successful

1. Specific organizational activities being focused on
2. Different kinds of organizational goals
3. Timely corrective action
4. Communication of the mechanics of the control process

Test Your Knowledge

Essay

1. List and discuss the three types of management control that are possible. (p. 428)

2. Describe the job of the controller. (p. 429)

3. Define total power and discuss the two different kinds of power. (p. 432)

4. List and discuss the four attitudes that a manager should attempt to develop in order to increase personal power. (p. 432)

5. List and discuss four specific areas which managers should take action to avoid potential barriers to successful controlling. (p. 433)

True-False

T F 1. Control is really quite arbitrary. (p. 422)

T F 2. Control is the last function of the four management functions. (p. 422)

T F 3. Controlling is the process that workers go through to control. (p. 422)

T F 4. One aspect of control is measuring performance. (p. 424)

T F 5. A standard can serve as a model. (p. 425)

T F 6. To bring the organization up to standard, symptom control is used. (p. 427)

T F 7. A symptom is a sign that a problem exists. (p. 427)

T F 8. Probably the best kind of control is feed-forward control. (p. 428)

T F 9. The controller is a line person. (p. 429)

T F 10. Power is influence. (p. 432)

Multiple Choice

1. Making something happen the way it was planned to happen is called _____. (p. 422)
   a. planning
   b. organizing
   c. leading
   d. controlling

Chapter Nineteen – Principles of Controlling

2. Controlling is the process that which group goes through to control? (p. 422)
   a. Workers
   b. Board of Directors
   c. Management
   d. None are correct

3. Which of the following is NOT one of the three main steps in the controlling process? (p. 423)
   a. measuring performance
   b. comparing measured performance to standards
   c. taking corrective action
   d. feedback control

4. Which of the following are parts of the control subsystem? (p. 423)
   a. Input
   b. Process
   c. Output
   d. All are correct

5. Two main measuring questions are _____. (p. 424)
   a. who and how
   b. how and what
   c. things and activities
   d. what and where

6. A standard is a level of activity established to serve as _____. (p. 425)
   a. model
   b. pattern
   c. design
   d. tool

7. Who was the focus at Marriott? (p. 425)
   a. Managers
   b. Waiters
   c. Bell persons
   d. Customers

8. A _____ is a sign that a problem exists. (p. 427)
   a. stereotype
   b. symptom
   c. signal
   d. None are correct

9. _____ are factors within an organization that are barriers to organizational goal attainment. (p. 427)
   a. Symptoms
   b. Corrective actions
   c. Problems
   d. Benefits

171

10. Probably the best kind of control is _____. (p. 428)
    a. feedback
    b. precontrol
    c. concurrent
    d. side-by-side

11. Which of the following is NOT one of the three types of management controls? (p. 428)
    a. Precontrol
    b. Concurrent control
    c. Feedback control
    d. Reflective control

12. _____ is control that takes place before some unit of work is actually performed. (p. 428)
    a. Precontrol
    b. Concurrent control
    c. Feedback control
    d. Reflective control

13. Control that takes place as some unit of work is being performed is called _____. (p. 428)
    a. precontrol
    b. concurrent control
    c. feedback control
    d. reflective control

14. _____ is control that takes place after some unit of work has been performed. (p. 428)
    a. Precontrol
    b. Concurrent control
    c. Feedback control
    d. Reflective control

15. If I want to find out how much control is needed, a good tool is _____ analysis. (p. 431)
    a. cost-ratio
    b. cost-benefit
    c. cost-proportion
    d. None are correct

16. What two types of power is total power based on? (p. 432)
    a. Organizational and customer
    b. Managerial and worker
    c. Position and personal
    d. Personal and professional

17. _____ is the extent to which an individual is able to influence others so that they respond to orders. (p. 432)
    a. Power
    b. Perception
    c. Value
    d. Beliefs

Chapter Nineteen – Principles of Controlling

18. The entire amount of power an individual in an organization possesses is called _____. (p. 432)
    a. the halo effect
    b. projection
    c. self-serving bias
    d. total power

19. _____ is power derived from the organizational position a manager holds. (p. 432)
    a. Position power
    b. Personal power
    c. Expert power
    d. Virtual power

20. The power derived from a manager's relationships with others is called _____. (p. 432)
    a. position power
    b. personal power
    c. expert power
    d. virtual power

Fill-In

1. _____ is managerial activity aimed at bringing organizational performance up to the level of performance standards. (p. 427)

2. Control that takes place before work is performed is called _____. (p. 428)

3. Managers using _____ create policies, procedures, and rules aimed at eliminating behavior that will cause undesirable results. (p. 428)

4. Managers exercising _____ are attempting to take corrective action by looking at organizational history over a specified time period. (p. 428)

5. The controller is also sometimes called the _____. (p. 429)

6. The staff person whose basic responsibility is to assist line managers with the controlling function by gathering appropriate information and generating necessary reports that reflect this information is called the _____. (p. 429)

7. The greater the ability an individual is able to influence others, the more _____ an individual is said to have. (p. 432)

8. _____ is power derived from the organizational position a manager holds. (p. 432)

9. Power derived from a manager's relationships with others is called _____. (p. 432)

10. _____ is generally enhanced by a move to a higher organizational position. (p. 432)

Chapter Nineteen – Principles of Controlling

Answers

Essay

1. The three types of management control that are possible include the following:
   a. **Precontrol** – control that takes place before some unit of work is actually performed. Managers using this type of control create policies, procedures, and rules aimed at eliminating behavior that will cause undesirable work results.
   b. **Concurrent control** – control that takes place as some unit of work is being performed. It relates not only to employee performance but also to such nonhuman areas as equipment performance and department appearance.
   c. **Feedback control** – control that takes place after some unit of work has been performed. Managers exercising this type of control are attempting to take corrective action by looking at organizational history over a specified time period.

2. The **controller** is the staff person whose basic responsibility is to assist line managers with the controlling function by gathering appropriate information and generating necessary reports that reflect this information. In smaller organizations, managers may be completely responsible for gathering information about various aspects of the organization and developing necessary reports based on this information. In medium- or large-sized companies, however, the controller handles much of this work.

3. **Total power** is the entire amount of power an individual in an organization possesses. It is made up of position power and personal power. **Position power** is power derived from the organizational position a manager holds. In general, a manager moving from lower-level management to upper-level management accrues more position power. **Personal power** is power derived from a manager's relationships with others.

4. The four attitudes that a manager should attempt to develop in order to increase personal power are:
   a. **A sense of obligation toward the manager** – if a manager succeeds in developing this sense of obligation, other organization members will allow the manager to influence them within certain limits
   b. **A belief that the manager possesses a high level of expertise within the organization** – in general, a manager's personal power increases as organization members perceive that the manager's level of expertise is increasing
   c. **A sense of identification with the manager** – the manager can strive to develop this identification by behaving in ways that other organization members respect and by espousing goals, values, and ideas commonly held by them
   d. **The perception that they are dependent on the manager** – the main strategy here is to clearly convey the amount of authority the manager has over organizational resources including those organization members personally receive in such forms as salaries and bonuses

5. The areas which managers should take action to avoid potential barriers to successful controlling include:
   a. **Long-term versus short-term production** – a manager, in striving to meet planned weekly production quotas, might be tempted to "push" machines in a particular area so hard they cannot be serviced properly.
   b. **Employee frustration and morale** – worker morale tends to be low when management exerts too much control. Employees become frustrated when they perceive management is too rigid in its thinking and will not allow them the freedom they need in order to do a good job.

Chapter Nineteen – Principles of Controlling

c. **Filling of reports** – employees may perceive that management is basing corrective action solely on department records with no regard for extenuating circumstances. If this is the case, they may feel pressured to falsify reports so that corrective action pertaining to their organizational unit will not be too drastic.
d. **Perspective of organization members** – although controls can be designed to focus on relatively narrow aspects of an organization, managers must remember to consider any prospective corrective action not only in relation to the specific activity being controlled but also in relation to all other organizational units.
e. **Means versus ends** – managers must keep in mind throughout the control process that the information gathering and report generating done to facilitate taking corrective action are activities that can be justified only if they yield some organizational benefit that exceeds the cost of performing them.

True-False

1. F
2. T
3. F
4. T
5. T
6. F
7. F
8. T
9. F
10. T

Multiple Choice

1. d
2. c
3. d
4. d
5. b
6. a
7. d
8. b
9. c
10. b
11. d
12. a
13. b
14. c
15. b
16. c
17. a
18. d
19. a
20. b

Fill-In

1. Corrective action
2. precontrol or feed-forward control
3. precontrol or feed-forward control
4. feedback control
5. comptroller
6. controller
7. power
8. Position power
9. personal power
10. Position power

Modern Management (9th ed.)
Part 6 - Controlling
Chapter Twenty – Production Management and Control

Overview

This chapter deals with the concepts of production, productivity, and quality. There is a presentation of the role of operations research, production systems, systems, processes, and operations control. Also included are insights on each concept.

Chapter Outline

Introductory Case: USAir Focuses on Turnaround to Build Productivity

I. PRODUCTION

   A. **Production control**—ensures that an organization produces goods and services as planned

   B. **Production** is defined as the transformation of organizational resources into products.

   C. **Productivity** is the relationship between the total amount of goods or services being produced (output) and the organizational resources needed to produce them (input).

   1. Some of the more traditional strategies for increasing productivity include:

      a. Improving the effectiveness of the organizational workforce through training
      b. Improving the production process through automation
      c. Improving product design to make products easier to assemble
      d. Improving the production facility by purchasing more modern equipment
      e. Improving the quality of workers hired to fill open positions

   D. Quality and Productivity

      1. **Quality** is the extent to which a product reliably does what it is intended to do.

         a. Focus on continual improvement
         b. Focus on quality and integrated systems

         c. **Quality assurance** is an operations process involving a broad group of activities that are aimed at achieving the organization's quality objectives.

            1. **Statistics quality control** is the process used to determine how many products should be inspected to calculate a probability that the total number of products will meet organizational quality standards.
            2. **"No rejects" philosophy** – although not economically feasible for most mass-produced products, emphasizing quality in the early stages will reduce rejects and production costs.

         d. **Quality circles**—small groups of workers that meet to discuss quality-related problems on a particular project and communicate their solutions to these problems to management at a formal presentation.

Chapter Twenty – Production Management and Control

E. Automation

1. **Robotics** is the study of the development and use of robots.

2. Strategies, systems, and processes

   a. A **strategy** is a plan of action.
   b. A **system** is a particular linking of organizational components that facilitates carrying out a process.
   c. A **process** is a flow of interrelated events toward a goal, purpose, or end.

II. OPERATIONS MANAGEMENT

A. **Operations management** is the systematic direction (strategy) and control of operations processes that transform resources into finished goods and services; it is getting things done by working with or through people.

B. Operations management considerations

1. Three key notions of operations management:

   a. Operations management involves managers
   b. Operations management takes place within the context of objectives and policies that drive the organization's strategic plans
   c. The criteria for judging the actions taken as a result of operations management are standards for effectiveness and efficiency

2. **Effectiveness** is the degree to which managers attain organizational objectives: "doing the right things."

3. **Efficiency** is the degree to which organizational resources contribute to productivity: "doing things right."

4. **Capacity strategy** is an operational plan of action aimed at providing the organization with the right facilities to produce the needed output at the right time.

   a. Five steps in capacity decisions:

   1. Measure the capacity of currently available facilities
   2. Estimate future capacity needs on the basis of demand forecasts
   3. Compare future capacity needs and available capacity to determine whether capacity must be increased or decreased
   4. Identify ways to accommodate long-range capacity changes (expansion or reduction)
   5. Select the best alternative based on quantitative and qualitative evaluation

Chapter Twenty – Production Management and Control

5. Location strategy

   a. Factors in a good location

      1. Nearness to market and distribution centers
      2. Nearness to vendors and resources
      3. Requirements of federal, state, and local governments
      4. The character of direct competition
      5. The degree of interaction with the rest of the corporation
      6. The quality and quantity of labor pools
      7. The environmental attractiveness of the area
      8. Taxes and financing requirements
      9. Existing and potential transportation
      10. The quality of utilities and services

6. **Product strategy** is an operational plan of action outlining which goods and services an organization will produce and market.

7. **Process strategy** is a plan of action outlining the means and methods the organization will use to transform resources into goods and services.

   a. Types of processes

      1. **Continuous process** – a product-oriented, high-volume, low-variety process used, for example, in producing chemicals, beer, and petroleum products.
      2. **Repetitive process** – a product-oriented production process that uses modules to produce items in large lots. This mass-production or assembly-line process is characteristic of the auto and appliance industries.
      3. **Job-shop process** – used to produce small lots of custom-designed products such as furniture. This high-variety, low-volume system includes the production of one-of-a-kind items as well as unit production.

8. **Layout strategy** is an operational plan that determines the location and flow of organizational resources around, into, and within production and service facilities.

   a. A **layout** is the overall arrangement of equipment, work areas, service areas, and storage areas within a facility that produces goods or provides services.

      1. A **product layout** is a layout designed to accommodate a limited number of different products that require high volumes, highly specialized equipment, and narrow employee skills.
      2. A **process (functional) layout** is a layout pattern based primarily on grouping together similar types of equipment.
      3. A **fixed-position layout** is a layout plan appropriate for organizations involved in a large number of different tasks that require low volumes, multipurpose equipment, and broad employee skills.

9. **Human resources strategy** – an operational plan to use the organization's human resources effectively and efficiently while maintaining or improving the quality of work life.

Chapter Twenty – Production Management and Control

        a. Operational tools in human resources strategy

           1. **Manpower planning** – an operational plan that focuses on hiring the right employees for a job and training them to be productive
           2. **Job design** – an operational plan that determines who will do a specific job and how and where the job will be done
           3. **Work methods analysis** – an operational tool used to improve productivity and ensure the safety of workers
           4. **Motion-study techniques** – operational tools that are used to improve productivity
           5. **Work measurement methods** – operational tools that are used to establish labor standards

III. OPERATIONS CONTROL

    A. **Operations control** is an operational plan that specifies the operational activities of an organization.

    B. **Just-in-time inventory**—control technique for reducing inventories to a minimum by arranging for production components to be delivered to the production facility "just in time" to be used.

        1. Best conditions for JIT

           a. In companies that manufacture relatively standardized products for which there is consistent demand

        2. Advantages of JIT

           a. Reduces the unnecessary labor expenses generated by manufacturing products that are not sold
           b. Minimizes the tying up of monetary resources in purchases of production-related materials that do not result in timely sales
           c. Helps management hold done inventory expenses

        3. Characteristics of JIT

           a. Closeness of suppliers – manufacturers using JIT find it beneficial to use raw materials suppliers who are based only a short distance from them
           b. High quality of materials purchased from suppliers – manufacturers using JIT find it especially difficult to overcome problems caused by defective materials
           c. Well-organized receiving and handling of materials purchased from suppliers – materials must be available for the production process where and when they are needed, because if they are not, extra costs will be built into the production process
           d. Strong management commitment – the system takes time and effort to plan, install, and improve. Therefore, management must be willing to commit funds to initiate the JIT system and to support it once it is functioning.

C. Maintenance control is aimed at keeping the organization's facility and equipment functioning at predetermined work levels.

1. Pure-preventative maintenance policy
2. Pure breakdown (repair) policy

D. Cost control is broad control aimed at keeping organizational costs at planned levels.

1. Four stages of cost control

    a. Establishing standard or planned cost amounts
    b. Measuring actual costs incurred
    c. Comparing planned costs to incurred costs
    d. Making changes to reduce actual costs to planned costs when necessary

E. Budgetary control

1. A **budget** is a control tool that outlines how funds are obtained and spent in a given period.

2. Potential pitfalls of budgets

    a. Placing too much emphasis on relatively insignificant organizational expenses
    b. Increasing budgeted expenses year after year without adequate information
    c. Ignoring the fact that budgets must be changed periodically

3. **Zero-based budgeting** requires managers to justify their entire budget request in detail rather than simply referring to budget amounts established in previous years.

4. A **variable budget** is one that outlines the levels of resources to be allocated for each organizational activity according to the level of production within the organization.

F. **Ratio analysis** is a control tool that summarizes the financial position of an organization calculating ratios based on various financial measures.

1. Four categories of ratios:

    a. Liquidity ratios
    b. Leverage ratios
    c. Activity ratios
    d. Profitability ratios

2. Using ratios to control organizations

    a. Managers should evaluate all ratios simultaneously.
    b. Managers should compare computed values for ratios in a specific organization with the values of industry averages for those ratios.
    c. Managers' use of ratios should incorporate trend analysis.

G. **Materials control** is an operational activity that determines the flow of materials from vendors through an operations system to customers.

1. Materials management activities can be broadly organized into six groups of functions:

    a. Purchasing
    b. Receiving
    c. Inventorying
    d. Floor controlling
    e. Trafficking
    f. Shipping and distribution

IV. SELECTED OPERATIONS CONTROL TOOLS

A. A control tool is a specific procedure or technique that presents pertinent organizational information in a way that helps managers to develop and implement an appropriate control strategy.

B. Using control tools to control organizations

C. Inspection – to inspect or not to inspect

D. Management by exception is a control tool that allows only significant deviations between planned and actual performance to be brought to a manager's attention.

E. Management by objectives

F. **Break-even analysis** is control tool that summarizes the various levels of profits or loss associated with various levels of productions

1. The basic ingredients of break-even analysis are:

    a. **Fixed costs** – expenses incurred by the organization regardless of the number of products produced.
    b. **Variable costs** – expenses that fluctuate with the number of products produced.
    c. **Total costs** – simply the sum of fixed and variable costs associated with production.
    d. **Total revenue** – all sales dollars accumulated from selling manufactured products or services. Total revenue increases as more products are sold.
    e. **Profits** – defined as the amount of total revenue that exceeds the total costs of producing the products sold.
    f. **Loss** – the amount of total costs of producing a product that exceeds the total revenue gained from selling the product.
    g. **Break-even point** – that level of production where the total revenue of an organization equals its total costs.

2. Types of break-even analysis

    a. Algebraic break-even analysis
    b. Graphic break-even analysis
    c. Control and break-even analysis

G. Other broad operations control tools

1. **Decision tree analysis** is a statistical and graphical multiphased decision-making technique that shows the sequence and interdependence of decisions.
2. **Process control** is a technique that assists in monitoring production processes.
3. **Value analysis** is a cost control and cost reduction technique that examines all the parts, materials, and functions of an operation.
4. **Computer-aided design (CAD)** is a computerized technique for designing new products or modifying existing ones.
5. **Computer-aided manufacturing (CAM)** is a technique that employs computers to plan and program equipment used in the production and inspection of manufactured items.

Test Your Knowledge

Essay

1. Discuss the three key notions that are conveyed by the concept of operations management. (p. 448)
2. List the five-step process that managers should follow to increase the likelihood of making sound strategic capacity decisions. (p. 450)
3. List and discuss the three basic types of layouts for manufacturing facilities. (p. 451)
4. List and discuss the three ways that managers should use ratio analysis to control. (p. 457)
5. List and discuss the seven major ingredients of break-even analysis. (p. 460)

True-False

T F 1. Production control is to ensure the organizational production of goods and services. (p. 442)

T F 2. Production is a limited process. (p. 442)

T F 3. Productivity includes the measurement of inputs and outputs. (p. 442)

T F 4. Sallie Mae used quality control circles to improve productivity. (p. 443)

T F 5. Quality assurance and a "no rejects" philosophy go well together. (p. 445)

T F 6. Quality circles were originally developed in Japan. (p. 446)

T F 7. Operations management is systematic. (p. 448)

T F 8. Layout strategy deals with structure. (p. 451)

T F 9. Motion-study techniques are part of human resources operational management. (p. 453)

T F 10. JIT stands for just inventory time. (p. 453)

Multiple Choice

1. _____ control ensures that an organization produces goods and services as planned. (p. 442)
   a. Human resources
   b. Process
   c. Production
   d. Quality

2. Production is what type of process? (p. 442)
   a. Transformation
   b. Slow
   c. Transmutation
   d. None are correct

3. Quality circles were originally developed in which country? (p. 446)
   a. China
   b. Germany
   c. USA
   d. Japan

4. Which of the following are parts of operations management? (p. 448)
   a. Selecting
   b. Designing
   c. Operating
   d. All are correct

5. _____ is the degree to which managers attain organizational objectives. (p. 449)
   a. Effectiveness
   b. Efficiency
   c. Reliability
   d. Validity

6. Which of the following is used to describe "doing the right things?" (p. 449)
   a. Efficiency
   b. Reliability
   c. Effectiveness
   d. Validity

7. _____ is an operational plan of action aimed at providing the organization with the right facilities to produce the needed output at the right time. (p. 449)
   a. Capacity strategy
   b. Location strategy
   c. Product strategy
   d. Process strategy

Chapter Twenty – Production Management and Control

8. An operational plan of action that provides the organization with a competitive location for its headquarters, manufacturing, services, and distribution activities is called _____. (p. 450)
   a. capacity strategy
   b. location strategy
   c. product strategy
   d. process strategy

9. _____ is an operational plan of action outlining which goods and services an organization will produce and market. (p. 450)
   a. Capacity strategy
   b. Location strategy
   c. Product strategy
   d. Process strategy

10. An operational plan of action outlining the means and methods the organization will use to transform resources into goods and services is called _____. (p. 451)
    a. capacity strategy
    b. location strategy
    c. product strategy
    d. process strategy

11. A(n) _____ is a layout designed to accommodate a limited number of different products that require high volumes, highly specialized equipment, and narrow employee skills. (p. 451)
    a. product layout
    b. process layout
    c. transitional layout
    d. fixed-position layout

12. A layout pattern based primarily on grouping together similar types of equipment is called a(n) _____. (p. 451)
    a. product layout
    b. process layout
    c. transitional layout
    d. fixed-position layout

13. A(n) _____ is a layout plan appropriate for organizations involved in a large number of different tasks that require low volumes, multipurpose equipment, and broad employee skills. (p. 451)
    a. product layout
    b. process layout
    c. transitional layout
    d. fixed-position layout

14. Which of the following is a type of process? (p. 451)
    a. Continuous
    b. Repetitive
    c. Job-shop
    d. All are correct

Chapter Twenty – Production Management and Control

15. _____ is an operational tool used to improve productivity and ensure the safety of the workers. (p. 453)
    a. Work measurement methods
    b. Work methods analysis
    c. Motion-study techniques
    d. Job design

16. JIT stands for _____. (p. 453)
    a. Just inventory timing
    b. Justice in training
    c. Just information technology
    d. Just in time

17. A budget is what type of tool? (p. 455)
    a. Financial analysis only
    b. Planning only
    c. Control
    d. None are correct

18. When only significant deviations are brought to the manager's attention, _____ is being practiced. (p. 459)
    a. MBO
    b. JIT
    c. Management by Exception
    d. Management by Exclusion

19. _____ are expenses incurred by the organization regardless of number of products produced. (p. 460)
    a. Fixed costs
    b. Variable costs
    c. Transitional costs
    d. Modular costs

20. Expenses that fluctuate with the number of products produced are called _____. (p. 460)
    a. fixed costs
    b. variable costs
    c. transitional costs
    d. modular costs

Fill-In

1. _____ is an operational plan that focuses on hiring the right employees for a job and training them to be productive. (p. 452)

2. Operational tools that are used to improve productivity are called _____. (p. 453)

3. _____ are operational tools that are used to establish labor standards. (p. 453)

4. _____ is a control tool that summarizes the financial position of an organization by calculating ratios based on various financial measures. (p. 456)

5. The sum of fixed costs and variable costs is called _____. (p. 460)

6. _____ is all sales dollars accumulated from selling the goods or services produced by the organization. (p. 460)

7. _____ are the amount of total revenue that exceeds total costs. (p. 460)

8. The amount of the total cost of producing a product that exceeds the total revenue gained from selling the product is called _____. (p. 460)

9. The _____ is that level of production where the total revenue of an organization equals its total costs. (p. 460)

10. _____ is a cost control and cost reduction technique that examines all the parts, materials, and functions of an operation. (p. 463)

Answers

Essay

1. The three key notions that are conveyed by the concept of operations management are:
   a. Operations management involves managers
   b. Operations management takes place within the context of objectives and policies that drive the organization's strategic plans
   c. The criteria for judging the actions taken as a result of operations management are standards for effectiveness and efficiency

2. The following is the five-step process that managers should follow to increase the likelihood of making sound strategic capacity decisions:
   a. Measure the capacity of currently available facilities
   b. Estimate future capacity needs on the basis of demand forecasts
   c. Compare future capacity needs and available capacity to determine whether capacity must be increased or decreased
   d. Identify ways to accommodate long-range capacity changes (expansion or reduction)
   e. Select the best alternative based on a quantitative and qualitative evaluation

3. The three basic types of layouts for manufacturing facilities include:
   a. **Product layout** –designed to accommodate a limited number of different products that require high volumes, highly specialized equipment, and narrow employee skills
   b. **Process layout** –based primarily on grouping together similar types of equipment
   c. **Fixed-position layout** –appropriate for organizations involved in a large number of different tasks that require low volumes, multipurpose equipment, and broad employee skills

4. The three ways that managers should use ratio analysis to control an organization are:
   a. Managers should evaluate all ratios simultaneously. This strategy ensures that they will develop and implement a control strategy appropriate for the organization as a whole rather than one that suits only one phase or segment of the organization.
   b. Managers should compare computed values for ratios in a specific organization with the values of industry averages for those ratios. Managers increase the probability of formulating and implementing appropriate control strategies when they compare their financial situation to that of competitors in this way.
   c. Manager's use of ratios should incorporate trend analysis. Managers must remember that any set of ratio values is actually only a determination of relationships that existed in a specified time period (often a year).

Chapter Twenty – Production Management and Control

5. <u>The major ingredients of break-even analysis include the following:</u>
   a. **Fixed costs** – expenses incurred by the organization regardless of the number of products produced. Some examples are real estate taxes, upkeep to the exterior of a business building, and interest expenses on money borrowed to finance the purchase of equipment.
   b. **Variable costs** – expenses that fluctuate with the number of products produced. Examples are cost of packing a product, costs of materials needed to make the product, and costs associated with packing products to prepare them for shipping.
   c. **Total costs** – simply the sum of fixed and variable costs associated with production.
   d. **Total revenue** – all sales dollars accumulated from selling manufactured products or services. Total revenue increases as more products are sold.
   e. **Profits** – defined as the amount of total revenue that exceeds the total costs of producing the products sold.
   f. **Loss** – the amount of total costs of producing a product that exceeds the total revenue gained from selling the product.
   g. **Break-even point** – that level of production where the total revenue of an organization equals its total costs. The point at which the organization is generating only enough revenue to cover its costs. The company is neither gaining a profit nor incurring a loss.

True-False

1. T	3. T	5. T	7. T	9. T
2. F	4. F	6. T	8. F	10. F

Multiple Choice

1. c	5. a	9. c	13. d	17. c
2. a	6. c	10. d	14. d	18. c
3. d	7. a	11. a	15. b	19. a
4. d	8. b	12. b	16. d	20. b

Fill-In

1. Manpower planning
2. motion-study techniques
3. Work measurement methods
4. Ratio analysis
5. total costs
6. Total revenue
7. Profits
8. loss
9. break-even point
10. Value analysis

Modern Management (9th ed.)
Part 6 - Controlling
Chapter Twenty One – Information Technology and the Internet

Overview

This chapter explores the relationship between information and data. MIS is explored, and a discussion of computers, networks, and the Internet is also included. Information about management decision support systems and how they operate is also presented.

Chapter Outline

Introductory Case: Making Changes Without the Right Information at Sunbeam?

I. ESSENTIALS OF INFORMATION

    A. **Data** are facts or statistics.

    B. **Information** is the set of conclusions derived from data analysis.

    C. Factors Influencing the Value of Information

        1. Four primary factors determine the value of information:

            a. **Information Appropriateness**—the degree to which information is relevant to the decision-making situation the manager faces
            b. **Information Quality**—the degree to which information presents reality
            c. **Information Timeliness**—the extent to which the receipt of information allows decisions to be made and action to be taken so that the organization can gain some benefit from possessing the information
            d. **Information Quantity**—the amount of decision-related information a manager possesses

    D. Evaluating Information

        1. Identifying and evaluating data
        2. Evaluating the cost of data

II. THE MANAGEMENT INFORMATION SYSTEM (MIS)

    A. A **management information system (MIS)** is defined as a network established in the organization to provide managers with information that will assist them in decision-making. An MIS gets information to where it is needed.

    B. Describing the MIS

        1. Six steps necessary to operate an MIS properly in order of their performance:

            a. Determining information needs
            b. Determining and gathering appropriate data
            c. Summarizing data
            d. Analyzing data
            e. Transmitting information
            f. Using the information

Chapter Twenty One – Information Technology and the Internet

        2. Different managers need different kinds of information—see Figure 21.4

    C. Establishing an MIS (involves four stages):

        1. Planning for the MIS – the planning stage is perhaps the most important stage of the process

        2. Designing the MIS (should consist of the following four steps):

            a. Defining various decisions that must be made to run an organization
            b. Determining the types of existing management policies that may influence the ways in which these decisions should be made
            c. Pinpointing the types of data needed to make these decisions
            d. Establishing a mechanism for gathering and appropriately processing the data to obtain needed information

        3. Implementing the MIS – making sure that the MIS is as simple as possible and serves the information needs of management is critical to a successful implementation of an MIS

        4. Improving the MIS – once the MIS is operating, MIS managers should continually strive to maximize its value

            a. Symptoms of inadequate MIS – operational, psychological, report content

            b. Answering questions such as the following helps MIS managers to determine MIS weaknesses.

                1. Where and how do managers get information?
                2. Can managers make better use of their contacts to get information?
                3. In what areas is managers' knowledge weakest, and how can managers be given information to minimize these weaknesses?
                4. Do managers tend to act before receiving information?
                5. Do managers wait so long for information that opportunities pass them by and the organization becomes bottlenecked?

        5. Typical Improvements to an MIS

            a. Building cooperation among MIS personnel and line managers
            b. Constantly stressing that MIS personnel should strive to accomplish the purpose of the MIS
            c. Holding, whenever possible, both line managers and MIS personnel accountable for MIS activities on a cost-benefit basis
            d. Operating an MIS in a "people-conscious" manner

III. INFORMATION TECHNOLOGY

    A. **Technology** consists of any type of equipment or process that organizational members use in the performance of their work.

B. **Information technology** is technology that focuses on the use of information in the performance of work.

C. Computer Assistance in Using Information

1. A **computer** is an electronic tool capable of accepting data, interpreting data, performing ordered operations on data, and reporting on the outcome of these operations. Computers are extremely helpful in generating information from raw data.

2. Main functions of computers

   a. **The input function** – computer activities through which the computer enters the data to be analyzed and the instructions to be followed to analyze the data appropriately
   b. **The storage function** – computer activities involved with retaining the material entered into the computer during the performance of the input function
   c. **The processing function** – computer activities involved with performing the logic and calculation steps necessary to analyze data appropriately
   d. **The control function** – computer activities that dictate the order in which other computer functions are performed
   e. **The output function** – computer activities that take the results of input, storage, processing, and control functions and transmit them outside the computer

3. Possible pitfalls in using computers

   a. Thinking that a computer is capable of independently performing creative activities
   b. Spending too much money on computer assistance
   c. Overestimating the value of computer output

IV. THE MANAGEMENT DECISION SUPPORT SYSTEM (MDSS)

A. **MDSS** is an interdependent set of computer-oriented decision aids that help managers make nonprogrammed decisions.

B. The following characteristics are typical of an MDSS:

1. One or more corporate databases

   a. A **database** is a reservoir of corporate facts consistently organized to fit the information needs of a variety of organizational members.

2. One or more user databases

   a. A **user database** is a database developed by an individual manager or other user.

3. A set of quantitative tools stored in a model base

   a. A **model base** is a collection of quantitative computer programs that can assist MDSS users in analyzing data within databases.

Chapter Twenty One – Information Technology and the Internet

    4. A dialogue capability

       a. A **dialogue capability** is the ability of an MDSS user to interact with an MDSS.

V. COMPUTER NETWORKS

    A. A **computer network** is a system of two or more connected computers that allows computer users to communicate, cooperate, and share resources.

    B. The **Local Area Network** is a computer network characterized by software that manages how information travels through cables to arrive at a number of connected single-user computer workstations.

    C. The **Internet** is a large interconnected network of computer networks linking people and computers all over the world via phone lines, satellites, and other telecommunications systems.

    D. The **World Wide Web** is a segment of the Internet that allows managers to have an information location called a **Web site** available continually to Internet users. Each Web site has a beginning page called a **home page**, and each home page generally has several supporting pages called **branch pages** that expand on the thoughts and ideas contained in the home page.

       1. A properly designed and used Web site is an organizational resource that can help managers reach organizational goals like the following:

         a. Marketing products more effectively
         b. Enhancing the quality of recruits to the organization
         c. Enhancing product quality
         d. Communicating globally
         e. Encouraging creativity in organization members

    E. **E-Mail** is a computerized information system that allows individuals the electronic capability to create, edit, and send messages to one another.

    F. **Intranets** are the internal corporate communications networks that use the structure and standards of the Internet to allow employees of a single firm to communicate and share information with each other electronically.

       1. An **extranet** is a program that allows outsiders to place orders and check the status of their orders.

Test Your Knowledge

Essay

1. List and discuss the four primary factors that determine the value of information. (p. 470)

2. Discuss four activities that have the potential of improving the MIS of most organizations. (p. 480)

Chapter Twenty One – Information Technology and the Internet

3. List and discuss the five main functions of computers in organizations. (p. 482)

4. List the five computer activities that dictate the order in which computer functions are performed according to the control function. (p. 483)

5. Discuss three major pitfalls that are possible in using computers to contribute to organizational success. (p. 483)

True-False

T F 1. Information is the set of conclusions derived from data analysis. (p. 470)

T F 2. Data are facts or statistics. (p. 470)

T F 3. MIS stands for Management Information Setup. (p. 474)

T F 4. MIS is usually a formally established organizational network. (p. 474)

T F 5. The primary function of MIS is to collect data. (p. 474)

T F 6. The first step in establishing an MIS is designing it. (p. 475)

T F 7. Technology is a specific type of equipment that impacts parts of the work world. (p. 481)

T F 8. One of the main functions of the computer is to store information. (p. 482)

T F 9. MDSS stands for Managerial Design Supplemental Service. (p. 484)

T F 10. A database is part of a MDSS. (p. 485)

Multiple Choice

1. What concept is described by the following: the set of conclusions derived from data analysis? (p. 470)
    a. Data
    b. Language
    c. Information
    d. Statistics

2. Which of the following influences the value of information? (p. 471)
    a. Appropriateness
    b. Quality
    c. Timeliness
    d. All are correct

3. Information _____ is the degree to which information is relevant to the decision-making situation the manager faces. (p. 471)
    a. appropriateness
    b. quality
    c. timeliness
    d. quantity

Chapter Twenty One – Information Technology and the Internet

4. The extent to which the receipt of information allows decisions to be made and action to be taken so the organization can gain some benefit from possessing the information is called information _____. (p. 472)
    a. appropriateness
    b. quality
    c. timeliness
    d. quantity

5. Information _____ is the amount of decision-related information a manager possesses. (p. 472)
    a. appropriateness
    b. quality
    c. timeliness
    d. quantity

6. What is the degree to which information represents reality? (p. 472)
    a. Timeliness
    b. Quality
    c. Quantity
    d. Appropriateness

7. The _____ is a network established within an organization to provide managers with information that will assist them in decision-making. (p. 474)
    a. Internet
    b. Extranet
    c. wide area network
    d. management information system

8. What is the first step in operating an MIS properly? (p. 475)
    a. Determining information needs
    b. Determining and gathering appropriate data
    c. Summarizing data
    d. Analyzing data

9. Which of the following is a stage in establishing an MIS? (p. 475)
    a. Planning
    b. Designing
    c. Implementing
    d. All are correct

10. Which of the following is a symptom of an inadequate MIS? (p. 480)
    a. Operational
    b. Psychological
    c. Report content
    d. All are correct

Chapter Twenty One – Information Technology and the Internet

11. Which of the following are main functions of computers? (p. 482)
    a. Input
    b. Output
    c. Control
    d. All are correct

12. The _____ of a computer consists of computer activities through which the computer enters the data to be analyzed and the instructions to be followed to analyze the data appropriately. (p. 482)
    a. input function
    b. storage function
    c. processing function
    d. control function

13. Computer activities involved with retaining the material entered into the computer during the performance of the input function describe the _____ of a computer. (p. 483)
    a. storage function
    b. processing function
    c. control function
    d. output function

14. The _____ of a computer involves computer activities that perform the logic and calculation steps necessary to analyze data appropriately. (p. 483)
    a. storage function
    b. processing function
    c. control function
    d. output function

15. Computer activities that dictate the order in which other computer functions are performed describe the _____ of a computer. (p. 483)
    a. storage function
    b. processing function
    c. control function
    d. output function

16. The _____ of a computer includes computer activities that take the results of input, storage, processing, and control functions and transmit them outside the computer. (p. 483)
    a. storage function
    b. processing function
    c. control function
    d. output function

17. MDSS stands for _____. (p. 484)
    a. Management Design Support Standby
    b. Management Decision Supplemental System
    c. Management Decision Support System
    d. None are correct

Chapter Twenty One – Information Technology and the Internet

18. A _____ database is developed by an individual manager or other user. (p. 485)
    a. user
    b. management
    c. CEO
    d. None are correct

19. LAN stands for _____. (p. 486)
    a. Local area network
    b. Location And Network
    c. Level and New
    d. None are correct

20. The _____ is a large interconnected network of computer networks linking people and computers all over the world via phone lines, satellites, and other telecommunications systems. (p. 486)
    a. intranet
    b. local area network
    c. Internet
    d. World Wide Web

Fill-In

1. _____ consists of any type of equipment or process that organization members use in the performance of their work. (p. 481)

2. Technology that focuses on the use of information in the performance of work is called _____. (p. 481)

3. A(n) _____ is a reservoir of corporate facts consistently organized to fit the information needs of a variety of organization members. (p. 485)

4. A collection of quantitative computer programs that can assist MDSS users in analyzing data within databases is called a(n) _____. (p. 485)

5. _____ is the simulation of a business situation over and over again, using somewhat different data for selected decision areas. (p. 485)

6. A(n) _____ is a system of two or more connected computers that allows computer users to communicate, cooperate, and share resources. (p. 486)

7. A computer network characterized by software that manages how information travels through cables to arrive at a number of connected single-user computer workstations is called a(n) _____. (p. 486)

8. _____ is a computerized information system that allows individuals the electronic capability to create, edit, and send messages to one another. (p. 490)

9. _____ are internal corporate communications networks that use structure and standards of the Internet to allow employees of a single firm to communicate and share information with each other electronically. (p. 491)

10. To give access to selected business partners, vendors, or clients, firms can expand their intranets with a(n) _____ program that allows outsiders to place orders and check the status of their orders. (p. 491)

Chapter Twenty One – Information Technology and the Internet

Answers

Essay

1. The four primary factors that determine the value of information are:
   a. **Information appropriateness** – the degree to which information is relevant to the decision-making situation the manager faces
   b. **Information quality** – the degree to which information represents reality
   c. **Information timeliness** – the extent to which the receipt of information allows decisions to be made and action to be taken so the organization can gain some benefit from possessing the information
   d. **Information quantity** – the amount of decision related information a manager possesses

2. The four activities that have the potential of improving the MIS of most organizations include:
   a. **Building cooperation among MIS personnel and line managers** – cooperation of this sort encourages lines managers to give MIS personnel honest opinions of the quality of information being received.
   b. **Consistently stressing that MIS personnel should strive to accomplish the purpose of the MIS** – providing managers with decision-related information – the better MIS personnel understand the decision situations that face operating managers, the higher the probability that MIS information will be appropriate for the decisions these managers must make.
   c. **Holding, whenever possible, both line managers and MIS personnel accountable for MIS activities on a cost-benefit basis** – this accountability reminds line managers and MIS personnel that the benefits the organization receives from MIS functions must exceed the costs.
   d. **Operating an MIS in a "people-conscious" manner** – an MIS is based on the assumption that organizational affairs can and should be handled in a completely logical manner. MIS activities should also take human considerations into account.

3. The five main functions of computers in organizations are as follows:
   a. **The input function** – computer activities through which the computer enters the data to be analyzed and the instructions to be followed to analyze the data appropriately
   b. **The storage function** – computer activities involved with retaining the material entered into the computer during the performance of the input function
   c. **The processing function** – computer activities involved with performing the logic and calculation steps necessary to analyze data appropriately
   d. **The control function** – computer activities that dictate the order in which other computer functions are performed
   e. **The output function** – computer activities that take the results of input, storage, processing, and control functions and transmit them outside the computer

4. The five computer activities include the following:
   a. When data should be retrieved after storage
   b. When and how the data should be analyzed
   c. If and when the data should be restored after analysis
   d. If and when additional data should be retrieved
   e. When output activities should begin and end

Chapter Twenty One – Information Technology and the Internet

5. The three major pitfalls that are possible in using computers to contribute to organizational success include:
   a. **Thinking that a computer is capable of independently performing creative activities** – a computer does not lessen the organization's need for a manager's personal creative ability and professional judgment. A computer is capable only of following precise and detailed instructions provided by the computer user.
   b. **Spending too much money on computer assistance** – managers need to keep comparing the benefits obtained from computer assistance with the cost of obtaining it. In essence, an investment in a computer should be expected to help the organization generate enough added revenue not only to finance the computer but also to contribute an acceptable level of net profit.
   c. **Overestimating the value of computer output** – managers must recognize that computer output is only as good as the quality of data and directions for analyzing the data that human beings have put into the computer. Inaccurate data or inappropriate computer instructions yield useless computer output.

True-False

1. T
2. T
3. F
4. T
5. F
6. F
7. F
8. T
9. F
10. T

Multiple Choice

1. c
2. d
3. a
4. c
5. d
6. b
7. d
8. a
9. d
10. d
11. d
12. a
13. a
14. b
15. c
16. d
17. c
18. a
19. a
20. c

Fill-In

1. Technology
2. information technology
3. database
4. model base
5. "What if" analysis
6. computer network
7. local area network
8. E-mail
9. Intranets
10. extranet

Modern Management (9th ed.)
Part 7 – Topics for Special Emphasis
Chapter Twenty Two – Competitiveness: Quality and Innovation

Overview

As most companies are discovering, the demand for quality and innovation are paramount to their ability to be competitive, and hopefully, successful. This chapter notes the relationship between quality and total quality management (TQM). It also points out the importance of quality as well as providing insights on how to provide quality. Also presented are strategic planning and its relationship to quality, as well as knowledge about the quality improvement process.

Chapter Outline

Introductory Case: LEGO's Mindstorms Market Research Causes Problem

I. FUNDAMENTALS OF QUALITY

    A. **Quality** is defined as the extent to which a product does what it is supposed to do—how closely and reliably it satisfies the specifications to which it is built.

    B. Defining Total Quality Management

        Total quality management is the continuous process of involving all organizational members in ensuring that every activity related to the production of goods or services has an appropriate role in establishing product quality.

    C. The Importance of Quality

        1. Offering high-quality goods and services typically results in three important ends for the organization:

            a. A positive company image
            b. Lower costs and higher market share
            c. Decreased product liability costs

    D. Established Quality Awards

        a. **The Deming Award** – the most prestigious international award
        b. **The Malcolm Baldrige National Quality Award** – the most widely known award in the United States

    E. Achieving Quality

        1. Crosby's Guidelines for Achieving Quality

            a. Integrity
            b. Systems
            c. Communications
            d. Operations
            e. Policies

2. Deming's Guidelines for Achieving Quality

   a. Create and publish to all employees a statement of the purposes of the organization
   b. Learn the new philosophy
   c. Understand the purpose of inspection
   d. End the practice of awarding business on the basis of price tag alone
   e. Improve constantly and forever the system of production and service
   f. Institute training
   g. Teach and institute leadership
   h. Drive out fear. Create trust. Create a climate for innovation.
   i. Organize the efforts of teams, groups, staff areas toward the purposes of the company
   j. Eliminate exhortations to the workforce
   k. Eliminate numerical quotas for production. Instead, learn and institute methods for improvement. Eliminate management by objectives. Instead, learn the capabilities of processes and how to improve them
   l. Remove barriers that rob people of pride of workmanship
   m. Encourage education and self-improvement for everyone
   n. Take action to accomplish the transformation

3. Juran's Guidelines for Achieving Quality—Mission-oriented

   a. The mission of the firm as a whole is to achieve and maintain high quality.
   b. The mission of individual departments within the firm is to achieve and maintain high quality.

4. Shingo's Guidelines for Achieving Quality—Poka Yoke

   a. The essence of **poka yoke** is that a production system should be made so mistake-proof that it is impossible for it to produce anything except good products.

5. Feigenbaum's Guidelines for Achieving Quality—Total Quality Management (TQM)

   a. The basic idea of **TQM** is that every operation in an organization can benefit from the application of quality improvement principles.

II. QUALITY THROUGH STRATEGIC PLANNING

   A. Environmental Analysis and Quality

   1. **Environmental analysis** is the study of the organizational environment to pinpoint factors that significantly influence organizational operations.
   2. Suppliers are often emphasized during environmental analysis by managers who stress quality.

   B. Establishing Organizational Direction and Quality

   1. In this step of the strategic management process, the results of the environmental analysis are used to determine the path that the organization will take in the future.

C. Strategy Formation and Quality

1. Management strategies that have proved especially successful in improving and maintaining high-quality operations and products include:

    a. Value adding
    b. Leadership
    c. Empowerment
    d. Partnering
    e. Gathering correct and timely information
    f. Continuous improvement

D. Strategy Implementation and Quality

1. Policies for Quality

    a. A **quality-oriented policy** is a standing plan that furnishes broad, general guidelines for channeling management thinking toward taking action consistent with reaching quality objectives.
    b. Quality-oriented policies can be made in virtually any organizational area.

2. Organized for Quality Improvement

    a. Juran suggests organizing a "quality council," consisting largely of upper managers, to direct and coordinate the company's quality improvement efforts.

E. Strategy Control and Quality

1. **Strategic control** emphasizes monitoring the strategic management process to make sure that it is operating properly.

2. Organizations go through five successive stages of quality maturity as they approach the maximum level of quality in all phases of organization activity.

    a. Uncertainty
    b. Awakening
    c. Enlightenment
    d. Wisdom
    e. Certainty

III. THE QUALITY IMPROVEMENT PROCESS

A. The Incremental Improvement Process

1. Step 1: An area of improvement is chosen, which often is called the improvement "theme"
2. Step 2: If a quality improvement team has not already been organized, one is organized
3. Step 3: The team "benchmarks" the best performers
4. Step 4: The team performs an analysis to find out how current performance can be improved to meet, or beat, the benchmark
5. Step 5: The team performs a pilot study to test the selected remedies to the problem
6. Step 6: Management implements the improvements

Chapter Twenty Two – Competitiveness: Quality and Innovation

B. Reengineering Improvements—Seven principles

1. Principle 1: Organize around outcomes, not tasks
2. Principle 2: Have those who use the output of the process perform the process
3. Principle 3: Subsume information-processing work into the real work that produces the information
4. Principle 4: Treat geographically dispersed resources as through they were centralized
5. Principle 5: Link parallel activities instead of integrating their results
6. Principle 6: Put the decision point where the work is performed and build control into the process
7. Principle 7: Capture information once and at the source

IV. INNOVATION AND CREATIVITY

A. **Innovation** is defined as the process of taking useful ideas and turning them into useful products, services, or methods of operation.

B. **Creativity** is defined as the ability to combine ideas in a unique way or to make useful associations among ideas.

C. Creativity in Individuals

1. Creativity is a function of three components:

   a. **Expertise** – everything individuals know and can do in the broad domain of their work
   b. **Creative thinking** – the capacity to put existing ideas together in new combinations
   c. **Motivation** – refers to an individual's need or passion to be creative

D. Encouraging Creativity in Organizational Members

1. Match individual expertise with work assignments
2. Provide resources necessary for creativity
3. Reward creativity

Test Your Knowledge

Essay

1. List seven of the fourteen points, according to Deming, that are necessary for a company (p. 503) to achieve a high level of success in improving and maintaining product quality.

2. Discuss four of the six strategies that have proved especially successful in improving (p. 507) and maintaining high-quality operations and products in organizations.

3. List and discuss the five successive stages that organizations go through as they (p. 509) approach the maximum level of quality in all phases of organizational activity.

4. List and describe the seven principles of reengineering. (p. 513)

5. List and discuss the three components of which creativity is a function. (p. 514)

Chapter Twenty Two – Competitiveness: Quality and Innovation

True-False

T F 1. Quality has always been the number one goal of American firms. (p. 500)

T F 2. TQM stands for Tremendous Quality Managers. (p. 500)

T F 3. The international award for quality is named for Juran. (p. 501)

T F 4. One of Deming's fourteen points is to drive out fear. (p. 503)

T F 5. Poka yoke roughly translates to quality management. (p. 505)

T F 6. A quality-oriented policy is a standing plan. (p. 509)

T F 7. In terms of the incremental improvement process, step one is often called the improvement theme. (p. 510)

T F 8. Bearings, Inc. uses the submissions to Quality Idea Briefs. (p. 512)

T F 9. Under reengineering improvements, the first principle is to organize outcomes. (p. 513)

T F 10. The seventh principle of reengineering is to capture information at the source. (p. 513)

Multiple Choice

1. What does TQM stand for? (p. 500)
   a. Tremendous Quality Methods
   b. Total Quantitative Measures
   c. Total Quality Management
   d. None are correct

2. Which of the following is a feature of quality? (p. 501)
   a. Image
   b. Lower costs
   c. Higher market share
   d. All are correct

3. Which of the following is the international quality award? (p. 502)
   a. Baldrige
   b. Juran
   c. Shingo
   d. Deming

4. Who among the following is noted for their work on quality? (p. 502)
   a. Shingo
   b. Deming
   c. Juran
   d. All are correct

5. According to Deming, top management has the primary responsibility of achieving _____. (p. 503)
   a. product quality
   b. product innovation
   c. employee satisfaction
   d. operation efficiency

Chapter Twenty Two – Competitiveness: Quality and Innovation

6. All of the following are part of Crosby's vaccination EXCEPT: (p. 504)
   a. Integrity
   b. Systems
   c. Operations
   d. Human resources

7. Which of the following is among Deming's 14 points? (p. 504)
   a. Eliminate exhortations to the workforce
   b. Encourage education and self-improvement for everyone
   c. Take action to accomplish the transformation
   d. All are correct

8. In Japanese, poka yoke means _____. (p. 505)
   a. Mistake-proofing
   b. Quality circles
   c. Management
   d. Worker

9. _____ is credited with originating the term total quality control, today often referred to as total quality management. (p. 505)
   a. Michael Porter
   b. Milton Freedman
   c. Armand Feigenbaum
   d. Geert Hofstede

10. The basic idea of _____ is that every operation in an organization can benefit from the application of quality improvement principles. (p. 505)
    a. operations management
    b. total quality management
    c. management information systems
    d. operations efficiency

11. The initial step in the strategic management process is _____. (p. 506)
    a. internal resource analysis
    b. environmental analysis
    c. downsizing
    d. reengineering

12. _____ is the study of the organizational environment to pinpoint factors that significantly influence organizational operations. (p. 506)
    a. Total quality management
    b. Critical path analysis
    c. Internal resource analysis
    d. Environmental analysis

13. A(n) _____ policy is a standing plan that furnishes general guidelines for channeling management thinking toward taking action consistent with reaching quality objectives. (p. 509)
    a. quality-oriented
    b. empowerment-oriented
    c. employee-oriented
    d. None are correct

Chapter Twenty Two – Competitiveness: Quality and Innovation

14. According to Crosby, organizations go through five successive stages of quality maturity. The first phase is _____. (p. 510)
    a. awakening
    b. enlightenment
    c. wisdom
    d. uncertainty

15. The first step in the incremental approach to improving quality is to _____. (p. 510)
    a. organize a quality improvement team
    b. identify benchmarks
    c. perform pilot study
    d. choose an area of improvement

16. _____ is the process of taking useful ideas and turning them into useful products, services, or methods of operations. (p. 514)
    a. Efficiency
    b. Effectiveness
    c. Innovation
    d. Specialization

17. The ability to combine ideas in a unique way or to make useful associations among ideas is called _____. (p. 514)
    a. Reengineering
    b. Creativity
    c. Standardization
    d. Effectiveness

18. _____ is everything an individual knows and can do in the broad domain of his or her work. (p. 515)
    a. Expertise
    b. Creative thinking
    c. Motivation
    d. Organizing

19. The capacity to put existing ideas together in new combinations is called _____. (p. 515)
    a. expertise
    b. creative thinking
    c. motivation
    d. organizing

20. _____ refers to an individual's need or passion to be creative. (p. 515)
    a. Expertise
    b. Creative thinking
    c. Motivation
    d. Organizing

Chapter Twenty Two – Competitiveness: Quality and Innovation

Fill-In

1. _____ is the extent to which a product does what it is supposed to do. (p. 500)

2. The most widely known award in the United States is the _____. (p. 502)

3. _____, who was originally trained as a statistician and began teaching statistical quality control in Japan shortly after World War II, is recognized internationally as a primary contributor to Japanese quality improvement programs. (p. 503)

4. _____ are often emphasized during environmental analysis by managers that stress quality. (p. 506)

5. A(n) _____ furnishes broad, general guidelines for channeling management thinking toward taking action consistent with reaching organizational objectives. (p. 509)

6. A standing plan that furnishes broad, general guidelines for channeling management thinking toward taking action consistent with reaching quality objectives is called a(n) _____. (p. 509)

7. _____ emphasizes monitoring the strategic management process to make sure that it is operating properly. (p. 509)

8. _____ is the ability to combine ideas in a unique way or to make useful associations among ideas. (p. 514)

9. The capacity to put existing ideas together in new combinations is called _____. (p. 515)

10. _____ refers to an individual's need or passion to be creative.

Answers

Essay

1. <u>Deming's fourteen points for improving and maintaining product quality are:</u>
    a. Create and publish to all employees a statement of the aims and purposes of the organization.
    b. Learn the new philosophy—this means top management and everybody else in the organization
    c. Understand the purpose of inspection—for improvement of processes and reduction of cost
    d. End the practice of awarding business on the basis of price tag alone
    e. Improve constantly and forever the system of production and service
    f. Institute training
    g. Teach and institute leadership
    h. Drive out fear. Create trust. Create a climate for innovation.
    i. Organize the efforts of teams, groups, staff areas toward the aims and purposes of the company
    j. Eliminate exhortations to the workforce
    k. Eliminate numerical quotas for production. Instead, learn and institute methods for improvement. Eliminate management by objectives. Instead, learn the capabilities of processes and how to improve them
    l. Remove barriers that rob people of pride of workmanship
    m. Encourage education and self-improvement for everyone
    n. Take action to accomplish the transformation

Chapter Twenty Two – Competitiveness: Quality and Innovation

2. <u>The six strategies that have proved successful in improving and maintaining high-quality operations and products in organizations are as follows:</u>
   a. **Value adding** – all assets and effort should directly add value to the product or service. All activities, processes, and costs that do not directly add value to the product should be eliminated because non-value-adding costs can be very wasteful.
   b. **Leadership** – in quality-focused organizations, "associates" are led. Management sets the organizational vision and values, and then works with the associates to perfect the production process.
   c. **Empowerment** – associates are organized into self-directed teams and empowered to do their jobs and even to change work processes if that will improve product quality. They are trained, retrained, and cross-trained in a variety of jobs.
   d. **Partnering** – the organization establishes "partnerships" with its suppliers and customers—that is, it actively works with them to find ways to improve the quality of its products and services.
   e. **Gathering correct and timely information** – the new global marketplace is exacting and unsympathetic. Managers no longer have time to wait for indirect traditional financial reports of performance to make the decisions required to compete successfully.
   f. **Continuous improvement and innovation** – the clarion themes of the quality movement are continuous improvement and constant innovation. Last year's best performance is not good enough today, and today's best practices will not be good enough perhaps even a month from now.

3. <u>The five stages that organizations go through as they approach the maximum level of quality in all phases of organizational activity are:</u>
   a. **Uncertainty** – there is no comprehension of quality as a management tool. Problems are fought as they occur, with ad hoc methods.
   b. **Awakening** – quality management is recognized as a valuable tool, but the organization is still unwilling to provide adequate resources to attack quality problems.
   c. **Enlightenment** – a quality improvement program is established. Top management becomes committed to the concept and implements all the steps necessary for the organization to face problems openly and resolve them in an orderly manner.
   d. **Wisdom** – management now thoroughly understands quality management. Quality problems are identified early, and employees are encouraged to suggest improvements to prevent defects from occurring.
   e. **Certainty** – quality management has become an essential part of the organization's system. Problems are almost always prevented, and quality improvement is a continuous activity.

4. <u>The seven principles of reengineering are as follows:</u>
   a. Principle 1: Organize around outcomes, not tasks
   b. Principle 2: Have those who use the output of the process perform the process
   c. Principle 3: Subsume information-processing work into the real work that produces the information
   d. Principle 4: Treat geographically dispersed resources as through they were centralized
   e. Principle 5: Link parallel activities instead of integrating their results
   f. Principle 6: Put the decision point where the work is performed and build control into the process
   g. Principle 7: Capture information once and at the source

Chapter Twenty Two – Competitiveness: Quality and Innovation

5. <u>The three components of which creativity is a functions include:</u>
   a. Expertise is everything an individual knows and can do in the broad domain of his or her work. This knowledge pertains to work-related techniques and procedures as well as a thorough understanding of overall work circumstances.
   b. Creative thinking is the capacity to put existing ideas together in new combinations. Overall, creative thinking determines how flexibly and imaginatively individuals approach problems. This capacity depends mainly on an individual's personality and work habits.
   c. Motivation refers to an individual's need or passion to be creative. Expertise and creative thinking are the individual's raw materials for being creative, but motivation determines whether or not an individual will actually be creative.

True-False

1. F
2. F
3. F
4. T
5. F
6. T
7. T
8. T
9. T
10. T

Multiple Choice

1. c
2. d
3. d
4. d
5. a
6. d
7. d
8. a
9. c
10. b
11. b
12. d
13. a
14. d
15. d
16. c
17. b
18. a
19. b
20. c

Fill-In

1. Quality
2. Malcolm Baldrige National Quality Award
3. W. Edwards Deming
4. Suppliers
5. standing plan
6. quality-oriented policy
7. Strategic control
8. Creativity
9. creative thinking
10. Motivation

Modern Management (9th ed.)
Part 7 – Topics for Special Emphasis
Chapter Twenty Three – Management's Digital Dimension

Overview

This chapter provides insights into how digital expertise and the digital environment relate to digital success, and discusses how digital dimensioning is similar to the strategic planning process. It also describes how digital dimensioning impacts the four primary activities of management. The six steps of the digital dimensioning process are also discussed in detail.

Chapter Outline

Introductory Case: Office Depot Recognized for Digital Excellence

I. DEFINING DIGITAL DIMENSIONING

    A. **Digital dimensioning** is the process of designing and implementing those digital activities that will best help a specific organization reach its goals.

    B. **E-business** is any organizational activity that is enhanced by an Internet initiative.

II. THE DIGITAL DIMENSIONING PROCESS

    A. The major steps in the digital dimensioning process include:

        1. Enlisting digital expertise – digital dimensioning activities will be successful only if individuals with appropriate skills perform them

            a. **Technical skills** that focus on the digital arena – the ability to use appropriately e-business hardware and software
            b. **People skills** that focus on the digital arena – the ability to influence people to become focused and involved in carrying out e-business activities
            c. **Conceptual skills** that focus on the digital arena – the ability to see the organization as a whole and design e-business activities to suit that view
            d. There are three primary options for managers who do not have sufficient digital experience in their organizations: (1) Management can train present organization members so that they develop needed digital expertise; (2) Management can hire new organization members who already possess the digital expertise; (3) Management can hire an e-business consultant.

        2. Analyzing the digital environment – the purpose of the analysis is to clearly define factors that can impact an organization's digital success not only in the present, but also in the future

        3. Establishing digital direction – this step can entail making digital direction tangible through a mission statement and related goals

        4. Formulating digital strategy – this step involves building a plan that outlines steps that the organization will take to reach its digital goals

5. Implementing digital strategy – in order to implement digital strategy successfully, managers must perform activities like allocating resources necessary to build systems required by digital strategy

6. Controlling digital dimensioning – this step essentially entails monitoring digital activities to ensure that digital goals are achieved

III. DIGITAL DIMENSIONING AND STRATEGIC PLANNING

A. **Strategic planning** is long-range planning that focuses on the organization as a whole.

B. Major strategic planning tasks include analyzing organizational environments, establishing organizational direction, formulating organizational strategy, and implementing the strategy and strategic control.

IV. DIGITAL DIMENSIONING: THE MANAGER'S WHOLE JOB?

A. Digital Dimensioning and Planning

1. **Planning** is the process of establishing organizational goals, choosing tasks that must be performed in order to reach those goals, outlining how the tasks should be performed, and determining when the tasks should be performed.
2. Through digital dimensioning, managers can establish tools to enhance the speed of gathering and analysis and the probability of making sound planning decisions.

B. Digital Dimensioning and Organizing

1. **Organizing** is the process of establishing orderly uses for all resources within an organization.
2. **Person-to-person collaborative tools** are Internet based applications that enable people to communicate from various locations in cities, states, or countries.
3. Overall, these tools help managers to gain maximum benefit from their greatest asset, the intelligence and expertise of their workers.

C. Digital Dimensioning and Influencing

1. **Influencing** is the process of guiding the activities of people in appropriate directions.
2. Management must keep in mind that how they influence others can impact the success of digital dimensioning efforts.

D. Digital Dimensioning and Controlling

1. **Controlling** is the process of making sure that events occur as planned.
2. Controlling can certainly impact the success of digital dimensioning.

Chapter Twenty Three – Management's Digital Dimension

Test Your Knowledge

Essay

1. List the six major steps involved in the digital dimensioning process. (p. 525)

2. Discuss the three skills necessary for individuals to possess in order for digital dimensioning activities to be successful. (p. 525)

3. Discuss the three primary options that are available to managers if they do not have sufficient digital expertise but want to enlist it in their organization. (p. 526)

4. Discuss the characteristics of controlling an organization's digital dimensioning activities. (p. 531)

5. Define person-to-person collaborative tools and give an example of how digital dimensioning can impact the organizing function of management. (p. 536)

True-False

T F 1. Establishing digital direction is the first step in the digital dimensioning process. (p. 525)

T F 2. Digital dimensioning activities will be successful only if individuals with appropriate skills perform them. (p. 525)

T F 3. Analyzing the digital environment involves monitoring, assessing, and making conclusions about organizational surroundings that could impact the success of the organization's digital efforts. (p. 527)

T F 4. The purpose of analyzing the digital environment is to clearly define factors that can impact an organization's digital success only in the present. (p. 527)

T F 5. Building on Michael Porter's ideas, one aspect of analyzing the digital environment involves monitoring it to determine the positive and negative impact that Internet activity is having. (p. 527)

T F 6. Once a manager has analyzed the digital environment of an organization, he or she is ready to build a strategy for reaching digital goals. (p. 530)

T F 7. Regardless of the validity of planned digital controlling improvements, the success of those improvements can be negatively influenced by their implementation. (p. 532)

T F 8. In organizations that do not have an established strategic planning process, digital dimensioning should be thought of as a substitute for strategic management. (p. 533)

T F 9. Digital dimensioning should be seen as a manager's entire job. (p. 534)

T F 10. Controlling is the process of guiding the activities of people in appropriate directions. (p. 536)

Chapter Twenty Three – Management's Digital Dimension

Multiple Choice

1. The latest feature of OfficeDepot.com is its new _____ capability. (p. 523)
   a. calculator
   b. inventory
   c. voice interaction
   d. distribution

2. _____ is the process of designing and implementing those digital activities that will best help a specific organization reach its goals. (p. 524)
   a. Digital dimensioning
   b. Strategic planning
   c. Operations management
   d. Perceptual mapping

3. Any organizational activity that is enhanced by an Internet initiative is called _____. (p. 524)
   a. networking
   b. digitizing
   c. E-business
   d. hypothesizing

4. Which of the following is the first step in the digital dimensioning process? (p. 525)
   a. Establishing digital direction
   b. Enlisting digital expertise
   c. Establishing digital direction
   d. Formulating digital strategy

5. Which of the following is the last step in the digital dimensioning process? (p. 525)
   a. Implementing digital strategy
   b. Establishing digital direction
   c. Formulating digital strategy
   d. Controlling digital dimensioning

6. Which of the following is NOT one of the skills necessary for digital dimensioning activities to be successful? (p. 525)
   a. Technical skill
   b. People skill
   c. Conceptual skill
   d. Virtual skill

7. _____ that focuses on the digital arena is the ability to use e-business hardware and software appropriately. (p. 525)
   a. Technical skill
   b. People skill
   c. Conceptual skill
   d. Virtual skill

Chapter Twenty Three – Management's Digital Dimension

8. Which of the following skills that focuses on the digital arena is the ability to influence people to become focused and involved in carrying out e-business activities? (p. 525)
   a. Technical skill
   b. People skill
   c. Conceptual skill
   d. Virtual skill

9. The aspect of _____ that focuses on the digital arena is the ability to see the organization as a whole and design e-business activities that suit that view. (p. 525)
   a. technical skill
   b. people skill
   c. conceptual skill
   d. virtual skill

10. Which of the following is NOT one of the three primary options available for managers who do not have sufficient digital expertise in their organizations but want to enlist it? (p. 526)
    a. Management can train present organization members so that they develop the needed digital expertise.
    b. Managers can hire new organization members who already possess the digital expertise.
    c. Management can enlist the needed digital expertise by hiring an e-business consultant.
    d. All of the selections are primary options available to managers to enlist digital expertise in their organizations.

11. According to _____, from the viewpoint of a specific manager, Internet activity can have both positive and negative impacts on the structure of an industry. (p. 527)
    a. Michael Porter
    b. Milton Freedmen
    c. W. Edwards Deming
    d. Geert Hofstede

12. _____ is the step that involves building a plan that outlines steps that the organization will take to reach its digital goals. (p. 530)
    a. Enlisting digital expertise
    b. Analyzing digital environment
    c. Formulating digital strategy
    d. Implementing digital strategy

13. Essentially, _____ entails monitoring digital activities to ensure that digital goals are achieved. (p. 531)
    a. enlisting digital expertise
    b. formulating digital strategy
    c. implementing digital strategy
    d. controlling digital dimensioning

14. Major strategic planning tasks include all of the following EXCEPT: (p. 532)
    a. establishing organizational direction
    b. formulating organizational strategy
    c. strategic control
    d. organizational feedback

212

Chapter Twenty Three – Management's Digital Dimension

15. Which of the following is NOT one of the four primary activities of management? (p. 534)
    a. planning
    b. organizing
    c. building
    d. controlling

16. _____ is the process of establishing organizational goals, choosing tasks that must be performed in order to reach those goals, and determining when the tasks should be performed. (p. 535)
    a. Planning
    b. Organizing
    c. Influencing
    d. Building

17. The process of establishing orderly uses for all resources within an organization is called _____. (p. 536)
    a. planning
    b. organizing
    c. influencing
    d. controlling

18. _____ is the process of guiding the activities of people in appropriate directions. (p. 536)
    a. Planning
    b. Organizing
    c. Influencing
    d. Controlling

19. Internet-based applications that enable people to communicate from various locations in cities, states, or countries are called _____. (p. 536)
    a. local area network tools
    b. person-to-person collaborative tools
    c. wide area network tools
    d. virtual reality

20. _____ is the process of making sure that events occur as planned. (p. 537)
    a. Building
    b. Organizing
    c. Influencing
    d. Controlling

Fill-In

1. The aspect of _____ that focuses on the digital arena is the ability to influence people to become focused and involved in carrying out e-business activities. (p. 525)

2. One illustration of positive impact on an industry is that by making the overall industry more efficient, the Internet _____ the size of the market. (p. 527)

3. _____ involves building a plan that outlines steps that the organization will take to reach its digital goals. (p. 530)

4. When _____ activities, managers must be aware that action taken to improve (p. 531) the effectiveness of digital activities should be monitored very carefully.

5. _____ is long-range planning that focuses on the organization as a whole. (p. 532)

6. Long term for strategic planning is usually defined as a period of time extending _____ into the future. (p. 532)

7. The process of establishing organizational goals, choosing tasks that must be performed in order to reach those goals, and determining when the tasks should be performed is called _____. (p. 535)

8. _____ is the process of establishing orderly uses for all resources within an organization. (p. 536)

9. The process of guiding the activities of people in appropriate directions is called _____. (p. 536)

10. _____ is the process of making sure that events occur as planned. (p. 537)

Answers

Essay

1. <u>The six steps of the digital dimensioning process are as follows:</u>
   a. Enlisting digital expertise
   b. Analyzing digital environment
   c. Establishing digital direction
   d. Formulating digital strategy
   e. Implementing digital strategy
   f. Controlling digital dimensioning

2. Like any organizational effort, digital dimensioning activities will be successful only if individuals with appropriate skills perform them. These skills relate to the digital arena and involve aspects of the technical skill, people skill, and conceptual skill. That aspect of **technical skill** that focuses on the digital arena is the ability to use e-business hardware and software appropriately, while that aspect of **people skill** that focuses on the digital arena is the ability to influence people to become focused and involved in carrying out e-business activities. That aspect of **conceptual skill** that focuses on the digital arena is the ability to see the organization as a whole and design e-business activities to suit that view.

3. If managers do not have sufficient digital expertise in their organizations, three primary options are available to enlist it. As the first option, management can train present organization members so that they develop needed digital expertise. A second option available is to hire new organization members who already possess the expertise. As a third option, management can enlist needed digital expertise in an organization by hiring an e-business consultant.

4. **Controlling** an organization's digital dimensioning activities is a special type of organizational control. This control focuses on monitoring and evaluating the digital dimensioning process to make sure that results materialize as planned. Essentially, controlling digital dimensioning entails monitoring digital activities to ensure that digital goals are achieved. While controlling digital dimensioning, if digital goals are not achieved, management might be required to take action like

improving digital strategy, improving how digital strategy is implemented, or reviewing the results of the analysis of digital environment to see if digital goals were set too high.

5. **Person-to-person collaborative tools** are Internet-based applications that enable people to communicate from various locations in cities, states, or countries. As an example of how digital dimensioning can impact the organizing function of management, digital dimensioning can be used to create ways to allow people to work together on specific projects from various locations around the world if necessary. More specifically, by employing person-to-person collaborative tools via the Internet, management can help people to work together as if they were in the same physical office.

True-False

1. F
2. T
3. T
4. F
5. T
6. T
7. T
8. F
9. F
10. T

Multiple Choice

1. c
2. a
3. c
4. b
5. d
6. d
7. a
8. c
9. c
10. d
11. a
12. c
13. d
14. d
15. c
16. a
17. b
18. c
19. b
20. d

Fill-In

1. people skill
2. expands
3. Formulating digital strategy
4. controlling digital dimensioning
5. Strategic planning
6. three to five years
7. planning
8. Organizing
9. influencing
10. Controlling